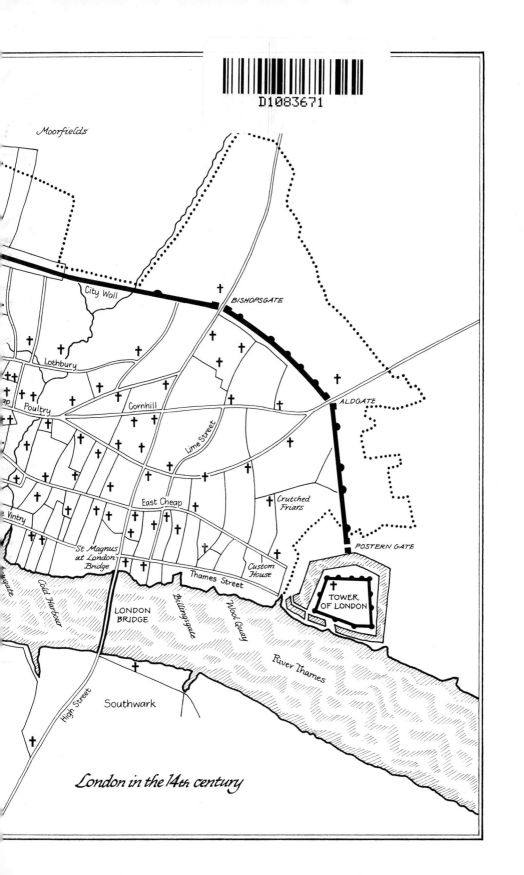

London in the 14th century

THE ENGLAND OF
PIERS PLOWMAN

WILLIAM LANGLAND AND
HIS VISION OF
THE FOURTEENTH CENTURY

THE ENGLAND OF
PIERS PLOWMAN

WILLIAM LANGLAND AND
HIS VISION OF
THE FOURTEENTH CENTURY

F. R. H. Du Boulay

D. S. BREWER

First published 1991 by D. S. Brewer, Cambridge

D. S. Brewer is an imprint of Boydell & Brewer Ltd
PO Box 9, Woodbridge, Suffolk IP12 3DF
and of Boydell & Brewer Inc.
PO Box 41026, Rochester, NY 14604, USA

ISBN 0 85991 312 0

British Library Cataloguing in Publication Data
Du Boulay, F. R. H. (Francis Robin Houssemayne) *1920–*
   The England of "Piers Plowman" : William Langland and his
vision of the fourteenth century.
   1. Poetry in English. Langland, William
   I. Title
   821.1
   ISBN 0-85991-312-0

Library of Congress Cataloging-in-Publication Data
Du Boulay, F. R. H.
   The England of Piers Plowman : William Langland and his vision
of the fourteenth century / F. R. H. Du Boulay.
      p.   cm.
   Includes bibliographical references and index.
   ISBN 0-85991-312-0 (hardback :alk. paper)
   1. Langland, William, 1330?–1400? Piers the Plowman.
   2. Langland, William, 1330?–1400?—Knowledge—England.
   3. England—Civilization—Medieval period, 1066–1485.
   4. England in literature.   5. Fourteenth century.   I. Title.
   PR2017.E5D8   1991
   821'.1—dc20   90-21711

This publication is printed on acid-free paper

Photoset by Rowland Phototypesetting Ltd
Bury St Edmunds, Suffolk

Printed in Great Britain by
St Edmundsbury Press Ltd, Bury St Edmunds, Suffolk

CONTENTS

ILLUSTRATIONS

The endpaper map is by Hilary Evans.

The plates appear between pp. 88 and 89

1. Receiving the tonsure from the bishop, whose clerk holds the Scriptures. British Library MS Harley Roll Y 6. English late twelfth-century.

2. Reaping under supervision. British Library MS Royal 2 B VII fo. 78b. English early fourteenth-century.

3. An early friar, supposedly St Francis, cutting out his own habit. British Library MS Yates Thompson 13 fo. 180v. English c.1325.

4. Moneybags. John Philpot, London alderman, d. by 1389. British Library MS Cotton Nero D VII fo. 105v.

5. Brew-house drinker. British Library MS Royal 10 E IV fo. 114b. English fourteenth-century.

6. English pilgrim. British Library MS Royal 17 C xxxviii. English fifteenth-century.

7. Friar hearing confession of a Poor Clare, his own penitential birch beside him. Bodleian MS Douce 131 fo. 126r. English or French c.1300.

8. Friars in the grip of devils. FitzRalph's treatise *De pauperie Salvatoris*. Corpus Christi College Cambridge MS 180 fo. 1r. English mid fourteenth-century.

9. Supposed bull of Pardons for Henry of Lancaster's helpers being read out in Canterbury Cathedral. c.1400. British Library MS Harley 1319 fo. 12a.

10. A young couple exchange marriage vows. Germanisches Nationalmuseum, Nuremberg, MS 4028 fo. 15r. South German c.1460.

ACKNOWLEDGEMENTS

Thanks are due to Professor John Burrow, who kindly read an early draft of this book and saved it from some errors. Encouragement and valuable criticism have also been given by Professor Hugh Lawrence, Professor Donald Logan and Dr Llinos Smith.

INTRODUCTION

Piers Plowman is the short and convenient title of one of the greatest English poems, written by a lanky and eccentric Midlander called William Langland. He was at work during the reigns of Edward III and Richard II (1327–99) and quite probably died in London before 1387.

After that for a hundred years or so a good many people heard the poem read or even read it themselves, and the number of surviving manuscripts (over 50) proves its popularity. Then it went out of fashion. The English language changed, and people found the text long and difficult.

Yet *Piers Plowman*, as a modern editor has written, 'in depth, intensity and richness of organization challenges comparison with works of the order of *Paradise Lost* and *The Divine Comedy*'.[1] It is full of ideas, scenes and images which bring to life an English past and at the same time speak to our own condition, which is not so different from that of fourteenth-century people as we sometimes like to think.

Geoffrey Chaucer, the other great poet of that age, is much better known, not least because *The Canterbury Tales* are rather easier to read in the original and have been popularized in musical production. It is easier, too, to laugh at neat and scurrilous stories than to follow through a single life's pilgrimage complex enough to puzzle a psychiatrist.

But Langland and Chaucer belonged to the same world. They were neighbours in London, acquainted with glittering courts, with poor people in cottages and with the crowds of passers-by, working, spending, drinking and dying.

So 'the vision of William Langland concerning Piers the Plowman and many other people' still deserves an audience, even if only through an

---

[1] A. V. C. Schmidt, *William Langland: the Vision of Piers Plowman* (Dent: Everyman's Library, revision of 1984), p. xvi.

introductory book like this, written by a historian who has been moved by the poetry and by the extraordinary story of a spiritual life in workaday surroundings.

We are often told in reputable text-books that the medieval period was at one and the same time an 'age of faith' and, in its later phase, an era of 'decay and corruption', particularly in the way the rich oppressed the poor and the Church did not live up to its ideals. In fact, Langland and Chaucer are themselves used as evidence for these notions in their satirical portrayal of money-grubbers and evil characters, often clergy, who battened on the ignorant and credulous.

These are half-truths. *Piers Plowman* is full of harsh criticisms of the world; but complaint is often a sign of health, especially when it is allied with self-criticism.

Certainly there were things wrong with both the Church and secular society. A great deal of time was given to managing church property and to refining the legal side of religion. Clergy were quite often avaricious and unchaste. Worst of all, perhaps, bishops and popes were involved in worldly politics including war and sometimes used spiritual weapons like ex-communication for secular purposes.

Against these accusations may be set the facts that the financial skills of the clerical world funded the great churches we still admire, and its legal skills provided reasoned solutions for many personal and public problems. Avarice and lechery are easily shown up in anecdotes and law cases but impossible to quantify, and they certainly do not disappear as we look backwards in time for some pure, remote age. As to political prelates, they have been with us since the times of the Apostles and even more so since the Emperor Constantine made Christianity licit (313). In Langland's youth the conventional piety of most Avignonese popes compares well with the murderous intrigues of eighth-century bishops of Rome or of the worldlings of the Renaissance.

Turning to English and European society in general, the lifetimes of Langland and Chaucer witnessed deadly epidemics and some years of famine and cruel warfare. On the other hand, the decline in the population improved the lot of the survivors. The warfare in England was intermittent and did not prevent the flourishing of trade and peaceful arts nor the creation of fortunes among commercial families. It was the betterment of conditions that roused simple people to a hatred of serfdom. To speak of the Peasants' Revolt of 1381 is to point to a unique event.

In short, Langland lived in a world of new complexity rather than new wickedness, and his articulate English, understandable across the land, is the hall-mark of the wonderful fourteenth century. His polemic against people who oppressed and deceived spilled over sometimes on to others, like the friars, whom we may think were fighting on the same side. But his spiritual and poetic power, valued by many of his contemporaries, ought to make despisers of the middle ages think more carefully.

'An age of faith' is a more tricky concept to deal with, both as a historical claim and as an idea which possesses exact meaning. In Langland's day practically everyone in England was a baptized Christian, and if many were credulous and superstitious they were not unconverted pagans as some French scholars would have us think. Richard Rolle, who lived in Langland's time, was fond of deploring his casual fellow-Christians, adding '. . . admittedly they go to church and even pack it to the doors'.[2]

The inner life of ordinary people can only ever be guessed at; but the survival of religious writings and pictures to be read, heard and seen suggests there was a substantial number of men and women who were accustomed to pray and meditate.

A difference between then and now, almost too obvious to mention, is the widespread assumption in the modern technological world that scientific knowledge has shown religion to be simply 'not true'. Molecular biology is a good current example because more detailed understanding of cerebral working and its evolution leads some distinguished scientists to discard the notion of 'mind' in favour of 'brain' and to deny the need for supposing an original Creator more complex than man. On the other hand many people in our own society, religion apart, have their own superstitions – horoscopes, charms, belief in spiritual vibrations, and the rest.

If we leave aside the general respectability of atheism amongst educated people in industrial societies, we are left with some striking similarities between the fourteenth and the twentieth centuries. In both there are intelligent and educated men who are believers and others of the same sort who are not. More important in terms of numbers, at both periods the mass of people lie somewhere in between total indifference to religion and an occasional hunger for personal consolation or cosmic meaning.

From the fourteenth century there is perfectly clear evidence that the population of baptized Christians contained men and women whose qualities and degrees of faith were extremely varied.

Richard Rolle (d.1349) could envisage a believing man married to an unbelieving woman.[3] Walter Hilton (d.1396) enumerates various types who made up the majority of nominal Christians in his time. They were the indifferent, the obstinate, the weak and also, some of them, actual sceptics, and among these, he continues, there are some who hold inwardly that there is no life of heaven, but do not say so outwardly.[4] The anonymous author of

[2] Richard Rolle, *The Fire of Love*, transl. Clifton Wolters (Penguin Classics, repr. of 1981), p. 50.

[3] *Ibid.*, chapter 24.

[4] Walter Hilton, *The Ladder of Perfection*, transl. Leo Sherley-Price (Penguin Classics, 1988), Book II, ch. 15; cf. chs. 7, 10.

The Cloud of Unknowing in the *Epistle of Privy Counsel* which he also wrote (late 14th century) referred to the intellectual society of his day as theologically blind: '. . . nowadays it is not just a handful but nearly everyone . . . who is blinded by subtle scholarship, theological or natural.'[5]

This is very much what Langland himself had to say in his pen-portrait of educated laymen at dinner mocking the idea of original sin and agreeing that human need for redemption was an unreasonable notion (B X 100–13). Nearer the beginning of his poem he placed a crucial passage about the irreligion of society: '. . . the majority of people who live and die on this earth find all that they value in this world and desire no better; they have no thought of another heaven' (B I 7–10).

These religious writers were no doubt making debating points about their native land, which they wished to convert, but their testimony carries conviction that numbers of men and women with some education were unbelievers at heart, while the majority of the simple and unlearned possessed what Hilton called a 'general belief', lacking in precision.[6] One of Langland's main contentions was the duty of the 'learned' to instruct the 'lewd' and especially to persuade people who would not otherwise have thought of it that to make interior acts of contrition during the year was better than waiting woodenly for Lent when Church rules said they had to go to confession anyhow and when the priest might be as ignorant as they into the bargain.

So *Piers Plowman* was and is an address to an unconverted world written by a man keenly aware that many people thought him a fool.

At the same time the poem, although designed to be read or recited, was a meditation made by the author to himself over a long period and doubtless again and again. It is not part of an artist's 'collected works', various in occasion and perhaps written to order like the 'newe thinges' Chaucer and court poets were sometimes asked for to celebrate royal and noble events.

The writing down of his meditations as a series of connected visions was none the less the work of a poet who betrays the deep solace he derived from poetry. It held him throughout his life. The poetry and the spiritual meditation were inseparable and long-lived.

Not surprisingly, *Piers Plowman* exists in several versions which show development in the poet's ideas. We can see him labouring at his text, starting, stopping, agonizing, altering and adding. We cannot help wondering how much of the final version was in Langland's thought when he first began.

The recent discovery of a single manuscript of early date has raised the

---

[5] *The Cloud of Unknowing & other works*, transl. Clifton Wolters (Penguin Classics, 1978, repr. of 1985), p. 163.
[6] Walter Hilton, *op.cit.*, Book II, ch. 10.

possibility of a fairly short first try: 1614 lines possibly written in the 1360s.[7]

The A text probably followed soon afterwards and took the story to some 2500 lines. Then after an apparent interval of self-doubt the B text thrust the vision forward through a series of profound 'dreams'. This may have been done in the 1370s. The C text, worked out but not completed before 1386, did not alter what the poet was trying to say but removed some obscurities and added fascinating passages where Langland appears to be saying something more personal about himself.

Some manuscripts show intermediate stages or mixed texts, so whoever did the copying must have had access to piecemeal revisions from the poet's writing quarters.

A book which is partly intended to serve as an introduction owes the reader a synopsis of the story. What follows makes no effort at detailed completeness nor to solve all the obscurities which continue to puzzle experienced scholars, for these can be studied at leisure (or not at all) without spoiling the impact of the whole. It is also taken for granted that a modern reader, accustomed to the subtle and allusive techniques of modern cinema, not to mention literature, will not be unduly bothered by the twists and turns of the episodes as they occur, or by the manner in which scenes dissolve into their successors and images replace one another.

It must be admitted at once that *Piers Plowman* is accepted as the poet left it, without any attempt in the present work to trace a development in his basic attitudes during the course of his writing. Such a task would be technical and tentative. It is enough to note here how Langland begins in the first four sections by looking at the political and social scene and then moves on progressively to the inner life of the individual. It is not exclusively a 'political' or a 'personal' poem for the modes are constantly mingling, and this should not be surprising in a Christian poet for whom men and women were both social beings, ideally bonded in a just order, and individual souls attempting to live in charity with God and their fellows.

The tone varies too: allegory comes alive through visual realism, sermonizing is interrupted by anguished argument, and the reader is sometimes stopped short by breath-taking lyricism. But the main story sweeps on as the poet-dreamer searches first for 'Truth', then for 'Do Well', and in the end for a Piers Plowman mysteriously transformed.

The poet falls asleep on the Malvern hills and dreams of the world, which is presented as 'a fair field full of folk' set between the tower of Truth on a hill to the east and the grim keep (donjon) of Falsehood ringed with dark ditches.

---

[7] A. G. Rigg and Charlotte Brewer (eds.), *William Langland. Piers Plowman: the Z version* (Pontifical Institute of Medieval Studies: Studies and Texts 59. Toronto, 1983).

The people in the world form a vast throng of the good and the bad going about their daily business. The poet had all the time in the world to decide who should lead his procession of people. It is worth identifying the leaders carefully, even at the cost of a slight disproportion of scale in this synopsis, because the first to appear carry much of the poem's meaning on their backs.

First are the ploughmen and farm labourers who work with little leisure, and they are paired by a group of characters in fine clothes who are doing nothing but showing off their persons. As 'winners' and 'wasters' they stand for a traditional theme in literature.

It is striking that these are followed by a tableau of those who remain stable in one place and those who are always on the move. Langland's first example is the hermit or anchorite who remains in the cell without hankering to roam about. These are points of recollected stillness to which the poet returns. But at once the scene jumps to a medley of people who, on the contrary, move restlessly about the country. Among an increasing number of fourteenth-century wayfarers, Langland chooses to point to merchants and minstrel-entertainers.

Langland was not completely dogmatic about such travellers. They numbered good and bad: honourable traders and cheats, innocent musicians and filthy comedians. Yet Langland shared a common medieval sense that the world was rightly ordered only when people followed their vocations, and that both aimless movement and unchecked numbers who lived by their wits were signs of folly and disorder. The world he saw was not going the right way, either in the behaviour of individuals or in the earth-tremors of a shifting society. Langland's mentality could only be happy with a society composed of ordered degrees and fixed numbers. The good monk ought to stay in his monastery; the true workman did not wander about begging; unlimited friars were a culpable folly, and there was something badly amiss when bondmen could flaunt wealth and position but sons of well-born fathers were reduced to menial life.

So the first dream-sequence announces the themes which will be repeated: stay settled, learn a craft, remain in your calling.

Commentators on *Piers Plowman* see it variously as a major landmark in the history of satire, a protest at a society that had gone wrong, or a prophecy of change in society to come. But to interpret Langland as a gifted critic is too limited. He was both less and more. He wrote of an age he did not always understand as well as we do, and it is historically justifiable to suggest that Langland's distress was caused partly by nostalgia for a past there never was. This explains the present book's attention in Chapters 2 and 3 to the changing world of the fourteenth century. They aim not to provide a generalized 'background' for the poem but rather a setting in which Langland's preoccupations and his own text can be clarified. Then, in the later parts of the book, Langland's poem is more directly used to explore his positive ideals of Christianity and how they might be served in a threatening world.

At the very outset, a beautiful woman comes down from the castle and speaks to the dreamer: 'are you awake, my son?' (She calls him Will in the C-text). 'Do you see all these people and how busy they are in their puzzled wanderings?' (B I 5–6).

It is Holy Church who speaks, and to her the poet 'cries out for grace' (B I 79), just as in the person of Conscience he will do again at the very end of the poem.

This early part of the work, sometimes called the *Visio* (not Langland's own title), surveys the community of men and women, both workers and wasters, under the king who is charged with ruling them. Into his court comes the richly-dressed figure of Lady Meed, who represents excessive worldly wealth, and the question arises whether she is to be married to Falsehood or Conscience. Conscience rejects her and the king at Westminster disowns her and promises to be advised in future only by Conscience and Reason.

The rôle given to the king and his court at Westminster (B II to IV) sometimes persuades readers that Langland was a political poet. This is only partly true, for after the opening scenes where the king observes and repudiates the venality and evil advice which plague his realm, attention turns decisively to the Christian interior life which it was the king's highest duty to safeguard by his just rule.

Yet it would be negligent to omit all mention of this political theatre which Langland observed from the wings. For him, as for historians today, the king's court, his council and the periodic larger assemblies called parliaments formed the centre of English political power. In Langland's day the court was the scene of troubles and scandals, but the problems were not fundamentally new ones. English kingship had existed in a state of tension for generations.

True enough, Edward III was losing his grip after his queen died in 1369. His finances were in ruins, his war in France an expensive fiasco, and Alice Perrers his mistress a symbol of greed and fiscal corruption.

But these were variations on an ancient theme. Royal government worked through a balancing act between the crowned monarch's undoubted right to rule as he pleased and the consent, at least tacit, of the great men of his land who were coming to be thought of as 'the community of the realm'. On the one hand stood the maxim of Roman Law, well-known to royal judges and implicitly accepted by simple people, that 'what pleases the prince has the force of law'. On the other hand was the historical fact that the king must rule in accordance with justice and by the advice of his 'natural counsellors' who were his nobles. A king who constantly refused co-operation found himself compelled.

The story had taken its familiar course from the Great Charter imposed on King John in 1215, through serious rebellions against Henry III and Edward II between the years 1258 and 1327, and so onward to Langland's England.

At every stage texts were written as charters, treaties, petitions, statutes and political songs to embody subjects' cries for justice and to insist that though the king might and must rule, he must do so according to law. The king might give what was his to whom he liked: lands, the guardianship and marriage of rich wards, pensions, assignments of customs revenues in return for loans, and so on. But he enriched upstarts or dispensed wealth through private and unaccustomed channels only at his peril. In Langland's day the king and his personal friends were loudly criticized, not least in the parliaments of 1376 and 1377. The petitions sometimes used the wording of complaints from the beginning of the century, but the speeches marked a new eloquence in parliamentary knights who were not hitherto known to be so politically vociferous. The future still lay with the great lords, by whom Richard II was ultimately undone, but that takes us past Langland's concern.

Langland's eloquence, however, provides a kind of linguistic parallel to the oratory in parliament we begin to hear in 1376. No closer coincidences can be proved. There is no evidence to identify Lady Meed with Alice Perrers, nor should we labour to show *Piers Plowman* as a manifesto of Langland's partisan disgust or even as proof of an unprecedented crisis. What was new was public articulation in English, and within the larger chorus of English voices Langland has a special place.

So the poem opens in this public way before working through to deeper and more individual themes. The transition may be seen in miniature in the character called Pees (Peace) who appears at the beginning (B IV) as a royal suitor presenting a bill, or petition, (as did hundreds of others) against the crimes of violence he had suffered. Such a petition might have been dealt with by the king himself or might have passed to one of his departments. The constitutional detail is irrelevant here, but the figure of Peace is not. From being a royal petitioner he changes in the course of the poem to the quality whose accepted poverty allows a traveller through the pass of Alton on the way to Winchester Fair without fear of robbery (B XIV 301). To Langland the traveller highway robbery provided more vivid poetic material than parliamentary petitions. It was an evil of public order epitomized by the Folvile gang of fourteenth-century Leicestershire (B XIX 248); it was a constant personal risk to a man of property like Peace, and it was also a Scriptural occasion on which a legendary character fell among thieves, not near Winchester but Jerusalem.

Piers Plowman is so often coloured by its opening scenes that space has been taken up in this synopsis to say that it is neither a merely political poem nor a merely personal one, but a spiritual text in which many of the world's affairs find a place.

As the Westminster scene dissolves the poem begins to concentrate on the dreamer's own turbulent passage through his life. In the last version (the C-text) he presents himself and tells – half confession and half apologia –

something like an indication of his own past. We must come back to this in the next chapter.

Meanwhile, a sermon is preached to all the people in the field by Reason. Public sermons were quite usual, and after this one the crowd was moved to repent, to confess, to mend their ways and make up by their reformed lives for what they had done wrong.

The momentum of the drama is kept up by these individual confessions of the people. By a neat device they are portrayed as the Seven Deadly Sins to which they are confessing. Although allegorical, each one is a sharply-drawn character who describes his or her mode of life in some detail. Langland was a keen observer and there can be few such vivid portraits from the medieval world, faces alight and gestures betraying their tricks (B V).

All the people decide to make satisfaction by setting out on a pilgrimage, not to some popular shrine in the customary way, half penance and half holiday, with a lot of sleazy hangers-on. Langland disapproved of that sort of thing. The preacher of the mission had directed them to somebody or something called Saint Truth whose identity is revealed gradually and cryptically.

The people are bewildered and don't know the way, and at that point Piers Plowman makes his first appearance:

> Peter! quod a Plowman, and putte forth his hed . . .   (B V 537)

> [By St Peter, said a ploughman, pushing his way through the crowd.]

Piers had half an acre, and although he gave a lot of directions for finding Truth, he decided to cultivate his field first and let the people help him before he set off as their guide (B VI).

It looked as though the pilgrimage was going to turn into a life of labour, earning a living honestly. But in a pivotal scene (B VII) Truth, who was being sought, suddenly granted a Pardon 'for Piers and his heirs for evermore', which would make sufficient satisfaction for their sins. Looked at closely this turned out to be not an ordinary papal or bishop's indulgence but a parchment bearing the bare statement that 'whoever does well shall go into eternal life and who does evil into eternal fire'.

This is one of the two great occasions in the poem when complicated or long-winded commandments are set down quite simply as the requirement to do good, which is to love God and neighbour. In this way a pilgrimage through space to a shrine of 'truth' is adroitly changed into a pilgrimage through time in the search for how to 'do well'.

The basic idea is simple, but the plot is made interesting through its very complexity; the reader may even feel invited to consider the sessions in personal terms.

Piers himself announces that his own plough shall be figurative and consist in reality in a life of prayer and penance. So Piers begins his mysterious transformation into a person of holiness. The poet, on the other hand, who tells us his adventures in a series of dreams, is someone we get to know as Will, and sets off in his simple russet coat on the long search for Do-Well. In one way he is any Christian, but the search appears increasingly like the poet Will's own personal experience.

The search occupies the long central part of the poem (B VIII to XV), up to the point where it turns more specifically into the search for Charity. In that typical medieval fashion which loved to divide up and describe things in significant numbers, especially in threes, it is arranged as the search for Do Well, Do Better and Do Best. These are not three distinct kinds of life but modes and degrees of the one good life, which is to love God and to love one's neighbour as oneself; so the major part of *Piers Plowman* is sometimes described as 'the Life' (*Vita*) in distinction from the earlier and shorter Vision.

The poet-dreamer's own life, occupied in looking for this love, or grace, has to be spent examining itself, not in self-admiration or egoistical intro- spection, but in careful questioning. The poet causes himself to meet a series of allegorical persons who stand for his own mental and spiritual faculties: Thought (B VIII), Intelligence (*Wit*) (B IX), Study, Sacred Learning (*Clergie*) and Scripture (B X), from all of whom he receives various instructions.

To these succeed Fortune and Nature who govern the mysterious opera- tions of the world where time brings the death and continued re-birth of living things. Problems and difficulties for the dreamer multiply, and they are problems about which others of his day also were anxious. What is the use of hard-won learning? Ignorant believers seem just as likely to make it to heaven, – 'To pierce heaven with a paternoster'. And why do some seem to win a place in heaven by some sudden act of submission after a lifetime's wrongdoing: the prostitute Mary Magdalen or the persecutor St Paul? And what about all those good people who had lived before the coming of Christ? Why, for that matter, was Adam allowed to ruin human happiness by an act of disobedience when all the rest of nature obeys the laws of its own being?

The age-old problems of the good non-Christian and the existence of evil take the dreamer to the brink of despair. Like so many others, he turns his back for a time on a life of effort which appears both demanding and unrewarding, and relaxes into the consolations which the world dispenses: the beguilement of a girl's admiring love, the security of personal possessions, and even a cultivated self-satisfaction ('pride of perfect living') (B XI).

It is an interlude. The dreamer is pulled up short, aware of critical eyes fastened on him. They are those of Imaginatif, a brilliant character who is another of the poet's own faculties (B XI 408ff.).

Imagination enables the mind to reach the invisible things it wishes to contemplate through the images of visible ones.[8]

In a section of great power the poet shows us himself as Imagination, brooding by himself over the years and receiving reproof, as it were from his *alter ego*, for dissolute ways and faithless ruminations –

> Are you not weary of ardent ways,
> Lure of the fallen seraphim . . . ?[9]

He argues with himself whether he should be writing poetry at all and muses about learning and intelligence, now thinking one thing, now another. Imagination offers so much metaphor and word-play that the dreamer awakes 'witlees nerhande' – almost out of his mind (B XIII 1).

At this point he dreams of his invitation to a dinner-party, which will be of crucial importance, for the guests are Scripture, Learning, a worldly doctor of divinity and, most specially, a wholly new figure, clothed obscurely as a pilgrim and called Patience.

Poised on the brink of spiritual transformation, however, the poet permits himself a digression. He introduces Haukyn, the Active Man (B XIII, XIV), who is in part a sketch of the dreamer himself[10] but exaggerated to form a contrast with Patience who has only just appeared. Haukyn is a man of the world, his coat stained with misdoings, his extravert voice loud with uncertainty. His rôle is to be persuaded by Patience that he too should seek Charity and that he especially should seek poverty. The idea is important because the whole poem is moving towards the praise of gladly-accepted poverty (the friars are a foil to this theme). But Langland seems to have thought the sequence too complicated, for in his last revision (the C-text) he understandably pruned it, and hastened the argument directly into Patience's teaching about poverty.

This is another of Langland's Christian paradoxes, radiantly relevant to his age of successful friars, sturdy vagabonds and poor women in hovels. Poverty, scourge of the fourteenth century, is extolled in a transposed key as the way to charity (B XIV).[11]

The shift from Imagination to Patience is basic to the teaching of *Piers Plowman*, because it marks the passage from the life of the mind to that of the soul. Hitherto the poet has been trying to use his brains. From now on he

---

[8] Britton J. Harwood, 'Imaginative in Piers Plowman', *Medium Aevum*, vol. 44 (1975), pp. 249–63.

[9] James Joyce, *Portrait of the Artist as a Young Man*.

[10] Stella Maguire, 'The significance of Haukyn, Activa Vita, in Piers Plowman', *Review of English Studies*, vol. 25 (1949), pp. 97–109.

[11] Geoffrey Shepherd, 'Poverty in Piers Plowman' in *Social Relations and Ideas: essays in honour of R. H. Hilton*, ed. T. H. Aston *et al.* (Cambridge, 1983), pp. 169–89, is a brilliant discussion.

thinks about spiritual faculties, which do not obliterate intelligence but illuminate it with wisdom.

The dreamer meets *Anima*, a name usually translated as 'soul'. In the C version it is given the more recognizable identification of 'free will', but in both texts the poet is bringing his dreamer into relationship with that principle of human self-hood known by various names according its apparently different aspects: life, mind, memory, reason, sense, conscience, love and spirit.

Not surprisingly, the discourse of *Anima* is about charity. In a burning phrase he (or she) carries the action forward by saying charity can never be recognized simply by appearances, but only by knowing the heart; and only one can do that – Piers the Plowman, *id est Christus*, that is, Christ.

It is characteristic of Langland that he should transform Piers in this mystical way, building up to the poem's climax, yet that he should also choose to lecture his hearers with a long inserted diatribe on proud priests and the right qualities of good ones (B XV).

The scene dissolves as *Anima* describes charity as a tree called Patience, and on the instant the tree appears. It grows from the heart of man, soil leased to one Free Will and tended in its growth under Piers the Plowman.

Here is a section where the images pour out in a torrent (B XVI). The tree's fruit are both charity and the souls of men and women who have been born since the world began, and they weep piteously at being plucked away into the Devil's keeping. One of them is Abraham, and the dream dissolves again into a swift pre-vision of Christ who will rescue them, and then the picture opens out into the long encounter with Abraham, Moses and the Good Samaritan, who stand for faith, hope and charity (B XVI, XVII).

Already the hearer or reader of the poem is long past the early troubled vision of fourteenth-century England and the introspections of the poet's youth, and is approaching the Passion of Christ and the unlocking of hell.

The images connect in many subtle ways. One particular train of ideas will serve as an example of Langland's intricate meditation. On the tree of charity the blossoms are said to be 'humble speech and gentle looks' (*benigne lokynge*) (B XVI 7); and although true charity in the heart can only be discerned by Piers-Christ, sweetness of facial expression was always for the poet a signal of the soul's love. So the idea of love or charity continues to be propelled forward by movements in the physical world. The tree's fruit are actual people, and three of them walk forward over the landscape: Abraham cradling those whom Christ will restore; Moses carrying the document of the Law which is simply 'Love God and love your neighbour', and the Good Samaritan on his way from Jericho to Jerusalem [*sic*] and his rescue of the man who had been injured by thieves.

If this seems to be a bewildering rush, a moment's reflection picks out the thread of meaning, which is charity or 'love'. It runs from the tree's blossoms which long like human souls for rescue, and thence to the protective arms of

Abraham; moving to Moses the complex Commandments of the Law are distilled into the absolute 'love your neighbour' (Lev. 19:18), and at the end of the narrative-thread the hand of the dismounted Samaritan stretches out to the pulse of the fallen traveller.

Of course there is more than that, but it need not detain a synopsis. A section of great power opens (B XVIII) as the sleeper dreams of Palm Sunday morning and the voices of children singing 'Glory, laud and honour' as the figure who looks like the Good Samaritan appears again, riding barefoot along the street.

We join the dreamer at the window looking out on to the crowds with Faith standing at his side who suddenly begins to shout, 'Hail, Son of David!' The figure on the colt's back blurs:

> Oon semblable to the Samaritan, and somdeel to Piers the
> Plowman . . .   (B XVIII 10)

[He looked like the Good Samaritan – or was it Piers the Plowman?]

'Isn't that Piers the Plowman?'
'No,' said Faith, 'it is the son of David come in chivalry to joust in Piers's arms – his helmet, coat of mail, his human nature.'

The climax is the crucifixion of Christ, told directly from the canonical and apocryphal Gospels without further reference to a jousting Piers, but in Langland's own luminous English:

> . . . Pitousliche and pale as a prison that deieth;
> The lord of lif and of light tho leide hise eighen togideres.
>   (B XVIII 58–9)

[He began to grow fearfully pale like a prisoner on the point of death. / And so the lord of life and of light there closed his eyes.]

This makes a natural climax to the drama built up from its beginnings in the fair field where all the world was milling round in search of the true way.

But William Langland did not see it like that, and whether we say he was confused, or subtle, or simple unable to stop composing, he makes in the two further sections the obvious points that the world goes on, the Church was founded, and the Church is in danger.

But as we read on it becomes clear that the artist and the prophet in the author have never been so close together. The puzzles which remain do not destroy the poem's structure or mask its lyricism, and the poet remains grimly alive.

After his death Christ is said in the apocryphal Gospel of Nicodemus to have rescued the God-fearing people of the Old Dispensation who had sat in darkness. The 'Harrowing of Hell' is told as a Christian triumph, and Langland in the telling celebrates poetry itself as part of man's natural happiness (B XVIII 410).

The building of the barn is the founding of the Church (B XIX 320f.) and mirrors the tower of Truth at the beginning of the poem, where the Church is given the form of the woman who walks down into the field. The cycle of evil and redemption seem on the verge of repetition. There is even a recapitulation of imagery. Just as at the beginning the great wind on a Saturday night had puffed trees to the earth with their roots in the air (B V 14–16), so now comes Antichrist

> . . . and al the crop of truthe
> Torned it so up-so-doun, and overtilte the roote . . .
> (B XX 53–4)

And the old enemies return.

There are different views about this ending of the story. Some read it as Langland's expectation of the world's last days and the dramatic coming of Antichrist in fulfilment of scriptural and medieval prophecies. Others see the poet's response to the ills of Christian society, or to his own old age. The alternative meanings will be discussed in the last chapter.

Whatever his anxieties, Langland brought extraordinary artistry to the depiction of his old age. Having written down the pilgrimage he had lived, he knew it could not be finished as long as he lived. The last dream is dreamed by a living Langland who hears Conscience decide, as he had once decided

> . . . I wole become a pilgrym
> And walken as wide as the worlde lasteth

and as Conscience cries out for grace the dreamer awakes.

Chapter 1

WILLIAM LANGLAND

Langland is known to us only through his long English poem, *Piers Plowman*, and if we want to understand him we have only the poem's texts to help us. To this challenging fact there are two small exceptions.

One is a marginal note in Latin written on one of the manuscripts in a handwriting of the early fifteenth century. It says that 'William de Langlond' made the book which is called Piers Plowman, and that his father was a gentleman (*generosus*) called Stacy (that is, Eustace) de Rokayle, who lived in Shipton-under-Wychwood in Oxfordshire as a tenant of the Lord Spencer.

The name Rokayle was not uncommon and occurs in enough records of the time to show there were Rokayles of modest substance in various parts of southern England.[1] Lord Spencer had some property near Malvern. Malvern, Worcestershire, in the west Midlands, was also the region from which Langland derived his dialect.[2] No other evidence gets us nearer to the poet's origin, and perhaps it does not matter. The note at least tells us independently who the author of *Piers Plowman* was, and it is now generally accepted.

The other external clue is, paradoxically, buried in the text, for there is a manuscript of the A version which contains a final and twelfth *Passus* before it breaks off. Langland (in my view) wrote much of this section, though he discarded it when he came to revise the poem; but its last ten or more lines are certainly spurious and were probably written by a certain John But, who was a royal messenger and died in 1387.[3]

---

[1] Oscar Cargill, 'The Langland Myth', *Proceedings of the Modern Language Association* (Baltimore), vol. 50 (1935). The argument here that William Langland himself is a myth is unconvincing.

[2] M. L. Samuels, 'Langland's Dialect', *Medium Aevum*, vol. 54 (1985), No. 2, pp. 232–47.

[3] The manuscript in question is Bodleian Library, Oxford, MS Rawlinson poet. 137. For this paragraph see Edith Rickert, 'John But, Messenger and Maker', *Modern Philology*, vol. 11 (1913), pp. 1–10; also George Kane, *Piers Plowman: the A Text* (London, 1960), p. 51.

These lines by John But say in effect that Will knew that what he had just been writing (in A XII) about holy life and the hope of heaven was profitable; also that he had written what appears in this manuscript, and also other works, about Piers the Plowman and many other people; and that when this had been done, before Will could look round, death dealt him a blow and felled him; the lines report that Will was buried and ask that Christ might receive his soul.

A few further lines indicate that it was John But who was saying this, and that as he too dabbled in poetry ('meddled with making') he thought he would have a go at rounding off what had been written in this early version. This seems to be a mildly teasing allusion to Langland's own self-mockery about 'meddling with making' instead of saying his Psalter (B XII 16).

Of course these are speculations, but they fit in quite nicely. Those last lines could hardly be by Langland apart from the question of their style, for there would be no point in Langland referring to his own death in that pious way as an accomplished fact. There is no reason to doubt the remarks were by John But, and since it has been shown that But died in 1387 it follows Langland himself was dead by then.

If we now move backwards in time to Langland's B text which the experts think was finished some time in the 1370s, we can read that he makes Imaginatif say to him 'I have been following you for five and forty winters' (B XII 3). It is not much to go on: medieval people were not very precise about numbers. But Imaginatif is supposed to be one of the poet-dreamer's own embodiments, so it is not unreasonable to suggest Langland was in his mid-forties in the mid-1370s. This reasoning gives us a conjectural, approximate span of 1330–1386 for William Langland's life.

If so, he would have been a slightly older contemporary of Geoffrey Chaucer. Strange as it may seem, there is no evidence they knew each other. Chaucer's circle of contacts can be gauged from many fragments of information which fill a large volume; but Langland is surrounded by blank space.

*   *   *

A consequence of Langland's obscure position is that we have to infer what he was like and what happened to him from his own writing. In doing this a historian must confess his own attitude to such a proceeding, because scholars themselves differ sharply over its legitimacy. Quite apart from modern theorists of literary criticism, some are minimalists who hold that the creator of a poetic fiction was in truth writing no more and no less than creative fiction. For them, the poet's apparent admission of his mode of life and work, his views and his relationships, are all placed out of the historian's reach by the writer's freedom of make-believe or his obedience to convention. Professor George Kane is severe on those who wish to deduce facts about the medieval author's life from his poetry, and although his criticisms in the case of Langland are directed against self-confident but undisciplined guesses, his ban is discouraging: 'We should not try to establish biographical possibilities'.[4]

Others, including the present writer, revere the poet for his imagination and creativity, yet hold that he can in a partial way be discerned through his own words. Even if he is being ironical or fanciful, it is a truism that he was working within a world he knew. Everything he wrote he must, be definition, have been able to think, and if he invented he could only do so within his conceptual world. So, for example, he may possibly not have lived in a cottage in Cornhill with wife and daughter, but his statement had meaning for him and, taken with other statements about London life, make it conceivable that Cornhill was at one time his address.

It is the same with literary borrowings. When Langland says heaven comes closest to earth in school and cloister, the learned objection that he was using an opinion borrowed ultimately from a long-dead religious writer does not automatically rule out some happy experience of Langland in school or cloister.[5]

The reader must ask himself why Langland said what he did in any particular context. In doing so, questions about the poet's stance, and therefore his life, present themselves irresistibly, especially with a poet like Langland who is evidently both observant about other people and opinionated about their conduct. The form of *Piers Plowman* and the additions to the C-text do not just permit speculation but demand it about this story-teller who dodged in and out of the first person. Always, of course, the student is left with the chance of his own error and the duty to be tentative.

In a curious way the lack of 'historical' evidence about Langland is an advantage. We have no option but to approach him through what he wrote. We cannot be side-tracked from the imaginative but real highroad of his life into paths littered with the concrete irrelevancies of mortgages or little fees paid for odd jobs. With all his reticence Langland responds well to this mode of enquiry precisely because he was introspective. His power of observation was of that sort. More interested in the interior than the external lives of human-kind, his Cornhill and Westminster remain shadowy while a drunken tavern-revel or a long look into a poor mother's living-room are communicated sharply.

*　　*　　*

[4] George Kane, *The Autobiographical Fallacy* (1965). For a sophisticated and also more positive view, see J. A. Burrow, 'Autobiographical Poetry in the Middle Ages', *Proceedings of the British Academy*, vol. 68 (1982), pp. 389–412.

A general reference of great importance for this chapter is E. Talbot Donaldson, *Piers Plowman: the C Text and its poet* (1949 and reprints).

[5] *Si paradisus in hoc mundo est, in claustro vel in scholis est* are words attributed to Petrus Ravennus, probably Peter Damian, by Benvenuto da Imola in his four-teenth-century commentary on Dante (R. E. Kaske, 'Langland and the *paradisus claustralis*', in *Modern Language Notes*, vol. 72 (1957), p. 482; cited by D. M. Murtaugh, *Piers Plowman and the Image of God* (Gainesville, Florida, 1978), p. 71 and n.

Piers Plowman is composed as a series of visions in which all kinds of people meet the dreamer and talk with him, and every so often he 'awakes' and writes his dream. Sometimes he puts himself into his dream as one of the actors being described by his waking self. For example, he tells how Piers is given a written Pardon and a priest appears offering to explain it, and while Piers is unfolding the document

> . . . I behind them both beheld all the bull . . .   (B VII 108)

In this way the author ensures that his audience is conscious of his identity.

It is only a short step to telling us his name, which he does quite early in the poem in the usual cryptic but conventional medieval way.

In the opening vision the lady comes down from the tower to the field and addresses the dreaming poet (in the C text) by name:

> . . . calde me by name
> And sayde, 'Wille, slepestou . . . ?'   (C I 4–5)

[She called me by name and said, 'Will, are you asleep?']

Even in the earlier recensions when he was less free with his personal details Langland offers plenty of clues, which were easy to manufacture with a name made for punning. (Only the evidence at the start of this chapter allays a suspicion the writer may have invented his own name.)

When he is looking for Do Well he writes

> Where Dowel . . . be in the land, our Will would know if wit
> could teach him   (A IX 116–8)

When repentance touches him he makes 'Will to weep water . . .' (C VI 2); and again, in his dissolute life wretchedness comes to him as a consequence 'for Will hath all his will' (C XII 1–2).

His second name is also conveyed without difficulty. 'I have lived in lond', quod I, 'my name is Longe Wille' (B XV 152), he told Anima, and he seems to be confessing also that 'Long' was a nickname, for 'I am too long, believe me, to stoop and endure work as a workman for any time' (C V 24); but if a nickname it sprang from the conjoined Long-lond.

Playing with words was part of the game, so while 'long' signified height 'longing' is made an allusion to the man's desire, and there is a connecting mockery between them. When Fortune carried the poet off into the evil ways of lust and avarice he is, so to say, ravished in an anagram 'into the land of longing' (B XI 8). So in the poet's mind there is a taint of licentiousness about being 'longland' and tall, just as there was with the false hermits tramping off on the Walsingham pilgrimage with their girl-friends – 'grete lobies and longe that loth were to swynke' (B Prol. 55).

*   *   *

If we had only William's tallness to put to his name, we could not go very far in knowing him. But he has allowed us a little more by adding some kind of personal confession about his earlier life to the last revision of his poem.

In the earlier versions Reason preached to the people and begged them to confess their sins. They responded by doing so, under the allegorical characters of the Seven Deadly Sins. It seems to have become desirable to the poet to join himself in with this general confession in a personal way. At any rate, in the last revision he inserted before Reason's sermon an apparent account of his own origins (C V 1–108), sometimes alluded to in cautious quotation-marks as the 'autobiographical' passage. It reads, with a particular intensity, as an explanation of his mode of life and his wish to redeem the time he had spent.

No paraphrase can convey the force of the poet's desire for this allowance of grace. But as the whole passage is full of ambiguities about his life's course it is best here to take his stages in a logical order, not his poetic one, and look at them a little more closely.

He began with his own origins. Years ago when I was a boy, he tells us, my father and my friends (meaning kinsfolk) provided the means to send me to school; and I have never found, since my friends died, any life that suited me better than the one in this long clerical dress.

As we have seen, William's father was a gentleman, for that is how the Latin *generosus* is always rendered in English from this time on. William was aware of his gentle origin, and for all his humility he stood firmly upon this social dignity. It was not a question of personal vanity but a consequence of the age's assumption that society was constituted in certain degrees.

If this idea of social 'degree' is hard to understand today, it was also becoming blurred in the fourteenth century, when new fortunes were being founded conspicuously while other families, proud of their ancient status, could be coming down in the world. Chaucer is an example of someone whose family had come to affluence through trade, Langland of a man who was not very successful in a worldly sense and was sensitive about it.

So after announcing his origin and vocation Langland goes off into one of his diatribes about his times: specifically, about bondmen's children being made bishops, shoemakers' sons being knighted for silver, and lords' sons becoming their labourers. He was insistent that the clergy should come from the families of 'franklins and free men' and be of legitimate birth.

'Franklin' was becoming a rather uncommon word for general use but for the poet's purpose it was near enough to the new-fangled 'gentleman' which described his own father. So Langland measured up to his own criteria for being a clerk. The pity was that his father and family who were paying for his education had died; their deaths may have put an end to his further clerical career. We don't know this, but only that he was against the thought that he should do manual work.

When he is discussing his youth and early vocation, Langland is even more vague than usual. But his whole poem shows without question that he was a subtle man and we must not take his obscurities as accidents. In fact, he gives us a possible clue.

In the 'autobiographical' section a number of comments are packed close together. He excuses himself from manual labour because he is too weak and too tall. Accused by Reason of able-bodied begging he simply answers that his education has given him the vocation to pray for the people who feed him (C V 22–52), and in a few minutes he confesses that although he has misspent his time like a man who has always lost in business he hopes at the last to receive a morsel of God's grace (C V 93–8).

Langland knew his Gospels well and in this very place refers to Luke 15:10 where the woman finds the coin which is the treasure of heaven. He cannot have failed to be thinking also of the next chapter; in Luke 16:1–8 occurs the famous parable in which the rich man dismisses his steward for not looking after his property. At his wits' end, the steward exclaims that he cannot dig and is ashamed to beg. The one chance of being taken back into his master's service is to call in those who owe his master debts and get them to pay. To each he offers a receipt for less than the full debt, and this is to forfeit his own commission. The master is pleased, and Christ speaks in the next few verses about receiving into eternal habitations those who cultivate a zeal for genuine riches.

It is hard to avoid the conclusion that Langland was tailoring his own life-story to the parable. Physical inability for manual labour is a thin excuse for this gentleman's son with a gift for preaching in poetry. His uneasy conscience about begging returns many times, but at least he is trying to persuade his Master's debtors to pay what they owe and hoping with great longing that the Master would favour him too even after his misspent time.

William Langland may well have been a tall man, as he suggests else-where. But the possibility of being a ploughman is unreal. He was lettered, knew it, and loved it. Something kept him from the priesthood and this we cannot know. The evidence for illegitimacy is very poor: apart from what he says about good birth, bastardy was easily dispensed anyhow. From behind his reticence he tells two things clearly: as a poet his solace in 'making', and as a Christian his wish to pay his master's debts and persuade his fellow-servants to do likewise.

There is no uncertainty about Langland's love of learning. His Latin literacy and his extraordinary ability in English went hand in hand, and he often reveals his gratitude at being schooled and made a clerk. Through the mouth of Imagination (B XII) he explains how a lettered man was like one in rough water who could swim: he meant that ability to read the sacred texts and to think about them helped a sinner to save himself from the flood of despair. He wrote also of the duty to help unlearned people by teaching them the same lessons of hope. More still, he could do all this through his own 'making', that is, his verses.

Reference is sometimes made to Langland's 'imperfect' training. His knowledge may well have derived from the liturgy and a few compendia such as Gregory the Great's *Moralia* and the *Golden Legend*. But as a criticism this is irrelevant. He had an adequate store of knowledge to feed the fire of his poetic genius and serve him as an educated Christian.

In a recurring motif, this precious sacred learning was 'the portion of my inheritance':

> Well may the child bless the one who educated him, for if he lives by the written word he may save his soul. *The Lord is the portion of my inheritance* [Ps. 15:5. Vulg.] is a cheerful verse.   (cf. B XII 187–9)

This was in fact the psalm used (and still is) in the Roman rite of making a boy or man a clerk, sung at the moment of snipping off the hair to give him the first tonsure.

The unanswerable question is where Langland received his relatively good education. He chose not to say. It is just possible he spent some time at Oxford and left without getting into any records. Young men with intense religious vocations sometimes abandoned formal schooling: Richard Rolle did so to become a hermit-writer and, like Langland, distrusted clever theologians; St Benedict himself had fled from the schools of Rome according to Gregory the Great.

Oxford would have been a perfectly possible place geographically for the Malvern boy to have attended while his family's support lasted. From some Master or formed Bachelor he could have learned the logical mode of disputing he displays in his poem:

> *Contra!* quoth I as a clerk and began the disputation . . .
>   (B VIII 20–6)

His mind was sharply trained. Familiar with a scholastic society where controversialists learned to pounce on each phrase of an authoritative text, he reminded his opponent in another place, not without irony, to read the whole passage before leaping to a deduction: 'Your quotation is quite correct, Madam,' he makes Conscience riposte Meed; 'You've discovered half the text but you need a scholar to turn over the page for you', and so he shows the proverb [Prov. 22:9 Vulg.] *He that giveth gifts winneth the victory* is concluded overleaf *but he taketh away the soul of him that receiveth them* (B III 338ff).

Later on the poet described how Dame Study had put *Clergie* to school and what she had taught him (B X 170ff): 'I put him to school', explained Dame Study, and went on to tell how she had instructed Scripture (wife of *Clergie*) in the Proverbs and the Psalter Commentary, logic and a certain amount of music. She rattled on in a rather general way about teaching both old philosophers and young children, and works up to warnings about

Theology, the only discipline to require charity as part of the learning process itself, and to words of grave doubt about astronomy, geometry and other parts of the Quadrivium, which shade into alchemy and sorcery, all of which are difficult and many of which are delusive.

These passages give a vague outline of the place of education and training in the world. The feminine gender of Dame Study and Scripture are, of course, purely fictive devices to explain the poet's views on the purpose of learning. We learn nothing here about Langland's own early experiences.

All we can be sure of is his selective knowledge of Scripture and his moral formation – 'what is best for body and soul as the Book teaches' (C V 38–9) – together with some acquaintanceship with scholastic techniques and a natural appetite for learning

> alle the sciences under sonne and alle the sotile craftes
>
> (B XV 48)

There were other and lesser skills too that Langland had likely enough gained. He was familiar at least in a general way with legal documents like conveyances, testaments and marriage contracts (B II 75ff, B XIV 189ff), though the appearance in the poem of stock phrases like *Sciant presentes et futuri* is no evidence that he was ever employed in writing out for a customer so much as a single deed.

He had some French too, or enough to incorporate a few proverbial lines. This was just at the time in England when knowledge of French was becoming dim, so that it had to be taught by masters who were paid by ambitious parents to lash the verbs into their pupils. Langland remarks 'French men and free men train their children to say "*Belle vertue est suffraunce . . .*"' (B XI 383ff. B X 436).

If William Langland did not join some kind of school at Oxford we can have no very strong clues about an alternative place of education. 'They found me to school', he wrote of his family, and elsewhere ruminated on 'the soul's ease' in cloister and in school where the dedicated clerk would find only affection (B X 298–302).

Aside from the Oxford possibility, editors have felt free to speculate, moving a finger uncertainly between his known locations of the Malvern hills and London. It has been noted that Great Malvern priory was a daughter-house of Westminster Abbey, though there is no record of a school there.

Yet it must be admitted that *Piers Plowman* contains faint hints that its author had experience, mainly happy, of life in a monastic school. If true, this would in no way imply he had been a monk in the making, for many religious houses at that time were offering board, lodging and education, usually in the monastic almonry, to sons of men willing to pay.[6] There are known instances at Worcester, Reading and elsewhere.

[6] Nicholas Orme, *English Schools in the Middle Ages* (1973), p. 243.

In the confession of Wrath, Langland makes him describe the penalties in a monastic chapter for telling tales: the accusation in front of the brethren, the whacking and the fasting (B V 167ff.). Later on, as we have seen, he contrasts the serenity and obedience of a monastic school as he seems to visualise it with an arrogant monk-landlord of the time he is writing (B X 299–310); and if the words were borrowed from an older author there would be little point in using them if the sentiment were not also Langland's.

Finally, in a passage which has attracted comment of various sorts, the poet entering his sixth vision hears boys and men singing the Palm Sunday antiphon: 'Glory, Laud and Honour'. The text reads

> Of gerlis and of *Gloria, laus* gretly me dremed
> And how osanna by organys olde folk songen . . .
> (B XVIII 7–8; C XX 6–7)

In general, the scene is of children and grown-ups singing together. In many larger monasteries there were singing boys to assist in the liturgy, and at Durham there is a specific record that there had been clerks singing in harmony, for which the word was *organum*, and helping the monks with the treble chant.[7] The lines above may therefore not be referring at all to an organ but be saying something like

> I dreamed vividly of children and older people
> singing 'Glory, Laud and Honour' in harmony . . .

There are difficulties: Langland's lines appear to make the grown-ups provide the harmony. But practice may have varied, or the poet may have been bending sense to the alliteration.

At all events, there are indications that Langland was familiar with the full Eastertide liturgy, which was doubtless performed in London, but also in some monastic churches elsewhere, and this is probably as far as we can go in supposing he himself might have experienced a monastic-school education.

Wherever Langland was educated, his natural abilities were plainly good enough to have earned him at least the Arts degree, and no impediment of birth, talent or personal distaste would seem to have stood between him and the priesthood. He revered the priesthood, however bitterly he attacked its unworthy members. So a further problem is why he settled into minor orders only, saying psalms and offices for the souls of his benefactors but never ordained to say Mass, hear confessions and preach to the people in his own church.

I think Langland tells us in a roundabout way. To put it briefly, he lacked patronage, and was unable to acquire a 'title'.

---

[7] *Ibid.*, pp. 245–6.

Canon law required that men who wanted to receive holy (major) orders from a bishop had to have a *titulus*, which is to say, a material assurance of a regular income to keep them decently and prevent them becoming a charge on the bishop or living in destitution. Every bishop's register shows this rule in operation. For a monk or friar who sought ordination, his *titulus* was his religious house or order. For secular or diocesan clergy, a 'title' was quite often provided by a religious house which had either got the patronage of parish churches in its gift and was thus able, as 'rector' to present a priest to one, or else was in possession of deposited funds from gifts and bequests, against which an ordinand's living could be guaranteed, possibly for some payment, not for the presentation (which would be simony and therefore illegal) but for the document.[8]

In the same way, an Oxford College or a lay patron might give a young ordinand his *titulus*. Occasionally a man of private means offered these as his guarantee, whereupon the bishop's registrar would record that he had been ordained 'to the title of his own patrimony, with which he is reputed to be content'.

This need of title for ordination and hence patronage runs right through English history. In the middle ages a young man might be granted a place as a pensionary clerk in a religious household with prospects of promotion.[9] In modern times a newly-ordained clergyman is sometimes said to 'serve his title' in his first parish.

Langland refers to this system when he criticizes those priests who take money for saying Mass or Offices even though they had received a title and therefore had no need for additional stipends:

> The title that ye take ordres by telleth ye be avaunced . . .
>
> (B XI 288–90)

> [The title by which you got your holy orders shows you have received preferment.]

In his 'autobiographical' passage he said, 'I never found since my kinsmen died a life that suited me better' and 'as I have to earn my living, I should do it in the way I have best learned'. It looks as if Langland had minor orders but never proceeded further because his family had died – perhaps of the plague – at a crucial point in his life, and the source of funds had gone. There may even have been other children with prior claims.

Now if Langland had been at the university he might well have done what other able but impecunious clerks could do: put his name down on one of the periodic lists (*matricula*) of graduates sent to the pope for provision to a benefice. This did not happen. Langland seems not to have had any

---

[8] A. Hamilton Thompson, *The English Clergy and their organization in the later middle ages* (1947), p. 143.

[9] W. A. Pantin, *The English Church in the Fourteenth Century* (1955), p. 33.

patronage let alone a degree, and he remained a man without worldly influence. Perhaps he was a difficult youth, eccentrically artistic, introspectively devout, or perhaps just unlucky.

These possibilities are increased by the trace of bitterness in his lines

> Popes and patrons pore gentel blood refused
> And taken Symondes sones seyntwarie to kepe . . . (C V 78–9)

> [Popes and patrons refused to help the sons of poor gentlemen but have accepted the sons of Simon Magus to have their own sanctuaries.]

He is simply saying in open language that a gentleman's son like himself did not get very far without papal provision or a patron in England, while those with money used it to obtain a title even though they were committing the sin of simony (buying spiritual gifts, cf. *Acts* 8) in acquiring a benefice and thus settling down in their own churches.

There is another oblique confirmation of this in a passage where Haukyn, a vehicle of Langland's views, complains that like other vagabonds he had never received anything from the pope, neither provender (= prebend) nor patronage, but only a piece of lead between two embossed heads or, in other words, a run-of-the-mill papal bull of pardon (B XIII 245). It may well be that even the crucial Pardon scene, and all the harshness of the poet's condemnation of those who took money for what was properly due only to those with pure intentions, gained force from a young man's disappointment.

* * *

One more problem about Langland's early life is that of his possible marriage. On two occasions he refers to a wife and once to a daughter whom he calls Kate and Calotte (C V 2; C XX 472). Some critics are sceptical and say that these names, alliteratively suitable, are quite common ones for fictitious women, and that their appearance in the poem may only be for dramatic effect.

This possibility must be admitted, though it seems less a disproof of Langland's marriage than a deliberate refusal on his part to give details of his family. If he was married we cannot say when. If he had a daughter we cannot say if she had brothers or sisters. It was an age of larger families than today, and the naming of a single daughter seems odd in more senses than one. Yet it is no more peculiar than to suppose William Langland was an only son. We can only admit ignorance.

For all that, it is hard after reading *Piers Plowman* to think of the poet as a lifelong celibate or even (to proffer a personal view) as a single man. It is not his obsession with legitimacy and monogamy that prompts this guess, for the fiercest upholders of sexual *mores* are sometimes the most crusty bachelors.

Likewise Langland was very hostile to marriage for the sake of property; so were many medieval commentators. Equally he protested against the easy nullity proceedings of the church courts; but there is nothing special about that either. Lollards also criticized church courts, not for prosecuting sexual offenders but for being too lenient, and Lollards favoured matrimony and the equal place of women.

What gives the sense of Langland as a married man is a kind of friendliness to the idea of happy marriage, and also of familiarity with the physical experience of marriage as opposed to short-term raptures.

'As for a maid who for a man's love leaves mother, father and kinsfolk, now such a one is worth loving' (C XVI 105–7), he wrote. 'She's much better than a girl got from a marriage-broker.' It's people like that, he said elsewhere, who keep the world going:

> In this world is Dowel trewe wedded libbynge folk,
> For their mote werche and wynne and the worlde sustene.
> (B IX 108–9)

> [It is faithful married folk who are the well-doers in the world, since they have to toil and produce and keep the world going.]

When we come to the course and style of love-making, too, Langland's perceptions are as keen as any other writer's, as he ticks off on his fingers, so to say, the devices (which he is deploring) of seduction: the little songs, the flirtatious glances, the fleeting touches, the tender promises.

> For ech a maide that he mette, he made hir a signe
> Semynge to synneward, and somtyme he gan taste
> Aboute the mouth or bynethe bigynneth to grope
> Til eitheres wille wexeth kene, and to the werke yeden . . .
> (B XIII 344–7)

> [For every girl he met he gave a suggestive signal, and sometimes kissed her intimately about the mouth or began to feel her lower down till they were aroused and went to work . . .]

But young experience is followed ruefully into age as he describes the worn husband whose wife asks more of his body than it can provide:

> For the lyme that she loued me fore and leef was to fele
> (A nyghtes, nameliche, when we naked were),
> Y ne myhte in none manere maken hit at here wille,
> So Elde and she hit hadde forbete.   (C XXII 195–8)

> [For that member she loved on me and liked to feel – night-times that is when we were naked – I could absolutely not make him

rouse up as she wanted, so much had old-age and she herself exhausted him.]

Passages like these suggest that Langland had an experienced and un-affected attitude towards physical sexuality. How far it can be made to fit into a biography is quite another matter. At one point he appears to confess a period of time when he accepted Fortune's offer of 'Lust-of-the-Flesh' (*Concupiscentia Carnis*). There is little remarkable about this except the vividness of the girl he describes (B XI 17ff.). But it leaves the reader without clue to the chronology of his marriage, if married he were.

At a mere guess, Langland remained a minor cleric because he could not get advancement to holy orders, and at some later time got married because he wanted to. This seems more likely than an early marriage debarring him from the priesthood, though we may consider the possibility. But whether married early or late or not at all, it is hard to see him, as some critics have, as a mismatched man. His paternalism towards the women ('Down on your knees') and little digs about their supposed inability to keep secrets are medieval common form.

*   *   *

After William Langland had written a considerable portion of the poem he apparently came to a temporary halt. This was probably in the late 1360s when he had been in London for some time, and what he had written is now called the A-text. At that point, and before he took up *Piers Plowman* again and carried it on to a conclusion in a revised way (the B-text) he seems to have suffered a spiritual crisis. This, already alluded to above in the Introduction, has been the subject of a perceptive argument by Professor J. A. Burrow.[10]

The poet's inner uncertainties may have coincided with serious illness, for the last piece of the A-text, later discarded by the author, refers to the visitation of Fever, allegorical messenger of death, who speaks to the poet, 'No, Will, go no further, but live as this life is ordained for you . . . and work towards Do Well while your days last, so that your joy may be great in Paradise' (A XII 89–95).

Whether Langland was himself ill or not, he had arrived in middle age at a tormenting impasse. In the early search for Do Well the dreamer had been made to hold discussions with Scripture and *Clergie* (that is, sacred learning) about the attainment of salvation. Behind the skilfully contrived disputes was a deeply sincere author who was writing his inmost troubles.

Put briefly, there were three obstacles to the continuance of his serene Christian hope. One was the divine arbitrariness in placing good men like

[10] J. A. Burrow, 'Langland Nel Mezzo del Camin', in *Medieval Studies for* J. A. W. Bennett (1981), pp. 21–44.

Solomon and Aristotle in hell while allowing entry into eternal happiness to
the penitent thief on the cross, to St Mary Magdalene and to St Paul, all of
whom had spent wicked lives but had repented suddenly. To an age which
visualized heaven with vivid realism as a place of eternal reward, the
prospect of this perfect compensation for most unequal work needed
explaining. It was a problem which worried other people at the time and it
occurs in the English poem *Pearl*, where the parable of the workers in the
vineyard who each get a penny at the end of the day is, not surprisingly,
referred to. One need hardly add that Langland's lack of originality in no
way lessens the actuality of the problem for him. His answers work themselves out in the texture of *Piers Plowman*.

The second difficulty was also about God's evident unpredictability,
namely, the supposed predestination of some and not others to heaven and
hence, presumably, the predestined relegation of the others to hell. To the
literal-minded who accept the occurrence of all things in time, an Almighty
who knows all things must know 'in advance' who will be saved and who lost;
and hence, as Langland put it, whether in this world he did wrong or not

> I was markid, without mercy and myn name entrid
> In the legende of life long er I were,
> Or elles undir-writen for wykkid . . .   (A XI 253–5)

> [I was marked without mercy, and my name entered in the Book
> of Life long before I existed, or else noted down as one of the
> wicked.]

This was another question which caused great anxiety to medieval people,
and Langland who arrived at a Christian answer kept the whole discussion
going in his last revision but put the speech attributing injustice to God into
the mouth of Recklessness.

The third difficulty was also a species of injustice, the evil which Langland
most hated, and it was the apparent futility of being learned when ignorant
men can easily get into heaven and scholarly men just as easily get plunged
down into hell. None are sooner saved, he wrote, than ploughmen and
shepherds:

> . . . swiche lewed juttes
> Percen with a Paternoster the paleys of hevene . . .
>   (A XI 301–2)

> [Such ignorant people penetrate with an Our Father the palace of
> heaven.]

Langland's perplexity in this matter was certainly not a feeling of superiority
over simple folk. He identified strongly with the common man, though he

argued that clerks had the duty of helping the unlearned by instructing them properly.

To the educated people of today, as indeed to professional medievalists of a generation ago, questions like predestination and divine rewards and punishments often seem meaningless and tedious; though perhaps in the late twentieth century physics and genetics may actually have brought the medievals a little closer by raising similar questions in another form.

However that may be, Langland found himself in bewilderment, real or contrived. His trouble was perhaps less of a formally philosophical nature than a deep diffidence about the course of his own life. He loved the world of learning which he thought of as 'the portion of my inheritance'. He was also a passionate writer of poetry, partly no doubt to communicate to others, but partly for himself as 'solace'. So he half-saw his own road to salvation as a kind of poeticized learning by which he was trying to understand and express love. Consequently the doubts about learning and about salvation itself were such as to cause anxiety.

The way the poem was going offered Langland no solution, and the problems that beset him probed at his weakest point, which was the maintenance of hope.

If indeed Langland experienced a crisis of middle life it was arguably one in which, hope faltering, he was open to hope's two enemies: blind presumption that all was well without effort or care – the extravert's answer; and the opposite reaction of despair – scourge of intraverts.

Despair was indeed a familiar word in Langland's vocabulary ('wanhope'), but at this point in his life it seems more likely from his text that he chose the other extreme, which was to smother doubts with delights.

He described in a particularly personal manner how he was 'ravished by Fortune into the land of longing and love' (B XI 7ff.). Fortune held up to him a mirror of the world and told him how he might see wonders and know that everything he desired might be his.

The first two temptations were in female form and were called Lust of the Flesh (*Concupiscencia Carnis*) and Covetousness of the Eyes. In their respective Latin and English forms the girls represented the sexual appetite conventionally supposed a peculiarity of youth, and the avarice or desire for possessions regarded even nowadays as the hall-mark of maturity.

There was, however, a third temptation, slipped in to the poem with such swiftness that it might almost be overlooked:

> Pride of Parfit Lyvynge pursued hem bothe,
> And bad me for my contenaunce acounten Clergie lighte.
>
> (B XI 15–16)

> [Pride in the Perfect Life hastened after these two and told me for the sake of my public appearance to be less concerned with sacred learning.]

and a little further on he wrote, 'pride of perfect living shall bring thee to much peril' (B XI 33).

A series of three temptations was familiar enough to strike a chord with the temptations of Christ in the wilderness at the start of his ministry (Mt. 4:1–10), but the echo here is remote. Now they correspond to the course of a life long lived and made to flash warningly upon the dreamer's inward eye. They were more likely to have been understood by the poet's hearers who were familiar with writings about the ages of man, like *The Parlement of the Thre Ages*.[11] But in Langland, as so often, the encounters are given a sharpness of outline that tempt us to suspect his own experience.

'You are a vigorous young man', said Langland's first apparition, throwing her arms round his neck. 'You have many more years to live and women to love.'

The flattery was irresistible, but within a page she has flitted away, and her place was taken by the more substantial consolation of possessions. She is the more complex one. At first blush avarice is presented as a small matter. She tells him not to worry:

> Have no conscience how thow come to goode . . .   (B XI 53)

or, if he felt a twinge as he feasted his eyes on the worldly possessions he could go and confess to a friar who would understand well enough.

But at second glance Langland's Covetousness of the Eyes was a much more serious proposition than a young man's lust, partly because she would stay with him a much longer time, partly because she obliterated more thoroughly his thought of Do Well, but also partly, it might be surmised, because lust was but an excess, so to speak, of the married love the dreamer legitimately had or might have, while avarice was a yearning for the secure possessions he then and always lacked, and not without bitterness.

As to the third temptation, it was sexless, spiritual and the most deadly, for it offered the seeker who had been bewildered and then wearied of erotic love and comfortable substance the very way he had been anxiously looking for: perfect living. But it was a way misdirected because it was not what it seemed to say.

From early till late the dreamer sought the habit of perfection. In his 'apologia' he would say in effect, 'Do not rebuke me, Reason, for in my conscience I know what Christ wants me to do: prayers of a *perfect* man and discreet penance is the work dearest to Our Lord' (C V 84). And of course he speaks not of moral perfection exactly but of the Gospel counsels of perfection ('if thou wilt be perfect, go sell . . .') The temptation was to be proud of this vocation and to condescend towards the clerical learning he could not yet properly value.

---

[11] J. A. Burrow, *The Ages of Man* (1986), esp. pp. 71–2.

It is a measure of Langland's complexity and self-knowledge that in writing these passages he already knew the temptation for what it was, and how to deal with it. In the next section Imagination will be made to enlighten and comfort the dreamer by saying, 'I noticed how you opposed learning with peevish words, and grumbled that the unlearned were saved more easily, but as a clerk you can understand the value of contrition even without confession; and this sort of knowledge comforts a clerk and *keeps him from despair.*' (B XII 176–9).

By the time the poet had overcome the disruption in his life and could write of what had happened, he was also able to show in what direction rescue lay. At the sweet words of abandon to Fortune he had forgotten like most men the flight of time and moved into old age, and Fortune left him, and poverty brought him low. Bewilderment and shame crush him until he meets Imagination.

This meeting with a vital faculty of his own person is one of the turning-points in the poet's life. Being a reflection of his own power, Imagination is native to him but only now recognized, suddenly and with gratitude:

> I have folwed thee, in feith, thise fyve and fourty winter . . .
>
> (B XII 3).

Langland was now writing again, and if we may hazard a guess, his taking up the poem and driving it forward towards Patience was made possible by renouncing the false hopes and fears of his younger manhood. A more sober imagination could picture the future.

'What do you think you are doing?' his other self asks. 'Amend while you may: you have been warned often enough. You have taken a beating, and the Psalter says "Thy rod and thy staff have comforted me." Why do you not go and say your Psalter instead of playing about with verses?'

> And thow medlest thee with makynges – and myghtest go seye
> thi Sauter . . .   (B XII 16)

This famous dialogue between the poet-dreamer and Imagination challenging the writer to abandon scribbling for a life of prayer may well express a real conflict. There is always a tension in Langland between art and contemplation. 'If only they would tell me', he cries, 'where Do Well . . . might be, I would indeed never work at this stuff but go pray all my life . . .'

But he is not told; his prayer was the poem, and we are the gainers. Never mind that his excuse was lame: it was surely meant to be. 'Somewhat me to excuse', he answered – and explained the writing of poetry as a solace for clerks (B XII 20–22); his implication is that the poetry and the search for Do Well are inseparable.

*   *   *

William Langland's life in London is of tantalising obscurity. Since he was an educated man, the question is whether this obscurity was chosen, and this in turn raises the problem of his livelihood.

He joined no noble household nor seemingly applied for the safe employment which his talents would have secured. If he had lived at even a modest social elevation in a conventional way, he would hardly have consorted with the idle loafing fellows about whom he wrote in both reproof and love. He purports to tell us that he lived in a cottage in Cornhill with wife and daughter, but if so we do not know when or for how long nor how he supported them.

The most familiar fact is his claim to have earned a living by reciting prayers, psalms and minor offices for the souls of those who helped him (C V 44–52). He expected to be fed by his friends, men and women, when he called during the month at their houses.

It is sometimes assumed that this sort of life was a perfectly usual one among minor clerics and, in a society which paid so much for prayers, not too difficult a way of getting some sort of livelihood. But quite apart from a hypothetical dependent family, Langland's life was probably fraught with mundane difficulties. Londoners of any means who were serious about their spiritual welfare mostly supported priests, either through chantries or fraternities,[12] to say Mass for them. Although parish clerks and other laymen were certainly given alms to recite subsidiary prayers like the penitential psalms or the Little Hours, the Mass as a sacrifice of propitiation was paramount. London was full of priests who could say Mass. The whole scheme of obits (prayers for the dead) implies that a man not in holy orders could have in it no full-time occupation, even though he could make a bit on the side with his psalter. Such a person would live precariously, even with other irregular employment which a literate might get. Langland refers to his Paternoster and his Primer,[13] and also, throughout his poem, to his poverty. The question of what he was doing will not go away, and perhaps a reasoned guess is possible.

It is well known that Langland frequently wrote about minstrels, sometimes in an approving sense and sometimes with bitter criticism. This contrast between the 'guiltless' and 'Judas's children' occurs in fact right at the start of the poem. But the most circumstantial account of such an

---

[12] Caroline M. Barron, 'The Parish Fraternities of Medieval London', in *The Church in pre-Reformation Society*, ed. Caroline Barron and Christopher Harper-Bill (1985), pp. 13–37.

Bequests to poor men to pray in a parish church were not uncommon. An example from St Andrews, Norwich, c.1500, specifies Vespers and Matins *if the men were learned* (N. P. Tanner, *The church in late medieval Norwich, 1370–1532* (Toronto, 1984), p. 104.

[13] For the Primer as a lay prayer book, see the classic paper in Edmund Bishop, *Liturgica Historica* (1918).

entertainer comes where the dreamer, in company with Patience and Conscience, meets the busy figure of Actif, otherwise known as Haukyn.

'I am a minstrel', he greets them, 'and I serve many lords'. Haukyn then explains some of the coarse numbers minstrels perform to entertain the well-to-do people who employ them, but he says that he himself is no good at that sort of thing. All he gets, he remarked wryly, is a blessing on Sundays when the priest asks the people to say an Our Father for Piers Plowman and those who desire his welfare (B XIII 224ff.). He adds that he sells wafers to all honest labourers.

This cryptic admission may make more sense if it is taken in the context of the poet's own life. Haukyn is not a portrait of the author – he is many-sided and composite – but he has something of Langland in him. Haukyn was also (among other things) a minstrel because the author made him one. There is no intention here to employ a circular argument and say that 'therefore' Langland was also a minstrel: there are signs he may have been, and these will be set out in a moment. But if we may be allowed to jump ahead and think of Langland as a minstrel, then some of Haukyn's features will enrich the image of the poet. In Haukyn we have a man who is no member of a regular household troupe like some minstrels, but serves, as he says, many lords and supplies wafers to all good workers. He is quite a poor fellow for whom the pope has done nothing, and there are vague references to a wife and children. But behind all his anxious activity is Haukyn's sense that with his hard work he provides something which is nourishing to honest men and women. Perhaps his wafers are a figure for the words of his mouth? He is present every Sunday when the priest leads the bidding prayers, and seems to direct his own prayers for Piers and all his helpers – 'For Piers the Plowman and that hym profit waiten . . .' (B XIII 237) – and after his good confession Conscience says 'no minstrel shall have more worth *than Haukyn wi[l] the wafrer*' (B XIV 28) who will receive dough even though no plough is at work, and it will be flour to feed people as is best for the soul.

These are speculations, but it is hard not to sense in Haukyn the supplier about the town of something more than bread, namely, the performances of a good minstrel who nourishes souls.

At this point we should look at minstrels. They were of many kinds of accomplishment and very much part of the medieval scene.[14] They are brought to life in a royal order of 6 August 1315 when Edward II's sheriffs in London and all over England were to try and cut down conspicuous expenditure in a year of famine. The number of courses served at lords' tables were to be reduced, and minstrels were to be forbidden to enter the houses of great lords without specific invitation – 'beyond three or four a day', the text adds with typical medieval vagueness. Those allowed in were to be satisfied with the food, drink and reward (*curtasie*) offered, and were

[14] Donaldson, *op.cit.* n. 4 above, chapter 5.

not to pester for more. Minstrels were not to go into the houses of lesser people at all unless asked.[15]

Even though this royal command was exceptional, it shows clearly the existence of a floating population of entertainers and servants (including messengers and archers) who were always on hand to press their services, whether wanted or not.

Household records of the king and great lords likewise show at all times in the medieval centuries that numerous companies of minstrels were employed.[16] At the lowest level they blended into the penumbra of suppliants sitting by the roadside, like those between Westminster Palace and Charing Cross who waited for alms in 1397 when the earl of Arundel was taken to execution after a well-publicized trial.[17] But moving up the scale we meet jugglers, story-tellers, musicians and poets. Texts speak of *fableur, narrator, conteor, disour, segger* or *joculator.* They were hired more or less informally, and paid in food, drink and money. Some were doubtless the retailers of *fabliaux*, the coarse stories which had been giving so much pleasure to courtly and urban audiences in France and England for the past couple of centuries.[18] Others were serious people who would recite the deeds of princes or lives of saints, and give 'solace to men in sickness or sadness'. In fact, the range of appeal was wide, from lowbrow knockabout to solemn edification.

If we now think back to the 'autobiographical' passages added to the poem towards the end of Langland's life, we may wonder again what he was doing as he wandered about in London and perhaps elsewhere, visiting people in their houses by invitation and receiving meals (C V 44–52). He only alludes to saying prayers for the souls of those who helped him, but it is more likely he did that in church, where he was a familiar attender. So did he go to his patrons' houses to pray? Must one envisage this minor cleric leading domestic prayers while the family sat round and gave him food afterwards? The picture is unconvincing, and it is easier to imagine him reading or reciting a *Passus* of his own poem. Later manuscript copies sometimes call *Piers Plowman* a tract, treatise, dialogue or vision and, divided for recitation into *Passus*, 'fitts' or sections, it was excellent material for edifying entertainment.

There are indeed a few positive hints that Langland was at some time a kind of godly minstrel. First, in the A-text, probably written in the 1360s, when he writes about teaching truth and love he says also that love is the

---

[15] *Calendar of Close Rolls. 1313–18* (HMSO, 1893), p. 306.
[16] T. F. Tout, *Chapters in medieval administrative history*, vol. 6, Index *s.v.* Minstrels. Now also Constance Bullock-Davies, *A Register of Royal and Baronial Domestic Minstrels, 1272–1327* (1988).
[17] Thomas of Walsingham, *Annales Ricardi Secundi* (Rolls series, 1865), p. 216.
[18] Charles Muscatine, *The Old French Fabliaux* (Yale, 1986).

plant of peace, and 'preach it during meal-time conviviality when they ask
you to sing, for by natural knowledge in the heart there begins a fitte' (A I
137–40).

Now, if we turn to the C-text, we find that at about the same time that
Langland added the 'autobiographical' piece, he also wrote a vivid section
dealing together with poverty, simple-minded beggars and God's minstrels
(C IX 70–161). The themes are closely interlinked and pursued with sharp
observation. Some beggars, he wrote, are apparently healthy but out of their
wits and wander about as the Apostles did, 'without bag and bread, as the
book telleth . . . and though they meet with the mayor in the street they do
not reverence him any more than anyone else': the reference is, of course, to
Luke 10:4: *carry no purse, no wallet . . . and salute no man on the way*. Such
people, Langland continues, may be minstrels of heaven, whom you should
invite home; you should welcome them and help them 'for they carry no bags
and bottles under their cloaks' (C IX 139). Here he is echoing the very words
he had written supposedly of himself (in C V 50): 'on this wise I beg, without
bag or bottle but my stomach alone'. He goes on immediately in Passus IX to
chide the idle vagabond, who feeds and warms himself by the hot coals,
stretches, drinks, sleeps, gets up when he likes, and wanders off on the
look-out for a round of bacon, money . . . or a lump of cheese, and so
saunters back with them to his cottage.

He seems unable to leave the subject alone. Soon afterwards he launches
into another attack, this time on unholy hermits (C IX 190ff.) who live on
rich men's alms but under false pretences because they are really only idlers
and drunks, quite unlike the holy solitaries of old who lived with the beasts in
wild places. The problem had troubled him ever since he began the poem,
for the third line of the earliest version tells how the poet began his
adventures by donning 'the habit of a hermit unholy of works'. One is
reminded of the young Richard Rolle cobbling together the garb of a
recluse; with Langland the misgivings were greater and more enduring.

As Langland listed the ways the good hermits of ancient days were
sustained, he seems to be also repeating his own self-questioning of Passus
C V. Here Conscience asked him whether he could labour or, if not,
whether he had lands to live by or 'lineage rich that find thee thy food . . . for
he seemed an idle man, living a lollarne lyf'. When the poet told how he had
been to school and got some learning by which he lived, Conscience retorted
that this was a strange sort of perfection – to beg in cities without being in a
religious order.

A striking mirror-image of these phrases appears in the lines C IX
195–200 which explains how some of the good hermits had livelihood of
their lineage, some laboured by learning or by their hands, and some had
friends in the world who brought them food: and although they were of 'high
kin', they had forsaken land and lordship and all the pleasures of the body.

The poet never told his hearers in plain language, but he leaves us with an echoing suspicion that he was himself a kind of holy entertainer, walking about on his visits and knocking at people's doors. Perhaps he offered the apostolic greeting, 'Peace be to this house' (Luke 10:5), with the chance of getting a welcome or not:

> And some lakked my lif – allowede it a fewe . . .   (B XV 4)

> [Some blamed my life, a few approved it]

and if he found friends he could go in, recite some part of his work, eat and drink, and so home till the next day of visiting or writing. The text does not forbid the drawing of such a man: peripatetic, mendicant, literate and of good family.

Langland certainly advised the world to support some of those who prayed for welcome. Rich men ought to be wary of taking in unseemly beggars, pretend fools, flatterers and liars, but should give their hospitality to three defined types: the poor, the handicapped, and the instructed man who would teach what Our Lord suffered 'and fiddle for you without flattery the Good Friday story' (B XIII 441–8; cf. C IX 134–7; C XI 31–34).

Every so often the reader finds himself wondering whether Langland's perception of the human struggle spills over into self-pity. Always insisting the life was his choice and vocation – 'the portion of my inheritance' – the poet spoke at moments of the hard and anxious round from Michaelmas to Michaelmas (B XIII 240), conscious of the passing years and the unfailing well-being of those the world favoured.

As Langland grew old in London, the sadness which informs and powers his poem seems to deepen yet, to do him justice, he treats his own decline less bitterly than the fate of the poor who had no reserves of poetry or learning to sustain them. 'I walked about like a beggar,' he wrote, 'often thinking how good fortune had deserted me at my most need, and how life was leaving me behind, vanishing with all my strength and good looks, and how . . .' (the sense flows on with hardly pause for breath) '. . . how friars followed folk who were rich, setting small price on people who were poor, nor giving resting-place in their church-yards to the corpses of poor common folk who in life had not paid them' (B XIII 2–10).

For himself, he had old age to occupy him but also his poem, and if in that connection we use the word 'consolation' it is only with the sort of justification and half-apology he himself had employed long since in the word 'solace'. Perhaps today that is a poor and pitiful sort of word, but to a medieval it signified happiness.

After thinking as best we can about William Langland's life, we have to wonder for whom he wrote, and why. These are separate questions, though allied, and if the one is difficult the other is of its nature speculative.

There are enough surviving manuscripts to show that the poem in all its forms had been copied and distributed within a generation of Langland's death into widely-spaced regions of England.[19] The diversity of speech and literary tradition in late medieval England, to which attention is rightly called, must not be thought so great that it prevented a common educated understanding. Just as London was 'linguistically tolerant' – how otherwise could people have understood all those England sermons, speeches and discussions? – so northern, midland and southern parts of the realm were receptive to the contents of the compendia and single manuscripts which instructed their readers about the past and the destiny of humankind and of English people in particular.

It is probably no more than a coincidence, but a telling one, that of the five *Piers Plowman* manuscripts whose one-time possessors are known, four were connected in some way with Yorkshire: a canon of York, a rector of Arncliffe in the Dales, a Londoner whose father or brother had come from Beverley, and a Speaker of the Commons, Sir Thomas Charlton, who was briefly taken as a prisoner to York during the civil wars of the fifteenth century. The manuscripts are not fine, expensive ones, and the poem is rather difficult. The owners, it may be surmised, thought of their copies as the possessions of serious, educated people, not the showy treasures of the really rich nor the technical tools of specialist scholars. In fact it is hard enough for us to classify work which is fictive, moral, spiritual and aesthetic all at once, written by an unqualified clerk who loved learning, a man of poetic genius who blushed a little for the way he spent his time, and an intense preacher of Christian love.

The character of Langland's audience has been inferred by experts from the manuscript tradition and does not form part of this general discussion of the poet himself. But it is linked to the motives for his writing. No one can presume to fathom these, yet one or two suggestions may be made.

By his own account the poet Langland was someone to whom unpleasant things happened. Of course, his misfortunes may have been exaggerated for effect. Getting yourself severely lectured in an autograph script is a common comic device. It is also a teaching method, and whatever else was in his mind Langland aimed to instruct. He also instructed in words of reasonableness and love, not by dreadful threats, as do so many religious preachers, despite a few plain words about the pains of hell (cf. B XIII 13).

Again by his own account he wrote to make some sort of a living even if only in the form of friendly hospitality from those who received him. At all events his audience was a good enough one to leave posterity a fair number of workmanlike copies.

---

[19] J. A. Burrow, 'The Audience of Piers Plowman', in *Anglia*, vol. 75 (1957), pp. 373–84, reprinted with postscript in *Essays on medieval literature* (1984), pp. 102–116; Anne Middleton, 'The Audience and Public of 'Piers Plowman', in *Medieval English Alliterative poetry and its literary background*, ed. David Lawton (1982), pp. 101–23.

Of course Langland's detailed intentions must strike the reader individually. But as he wrote about his own age with the pen of a critical Christian his work is a historical source to be treasured. He also admitted he was doing something else as well. When challenged by Imagination with wasting his time, he answered that he understood the objection quite well but that Cato, a man of learning, still approved of poetry as a solace, 'just as I do', and even the holy men of the past had found recreation a help towards perfection (B XII 20–24).

If the John But we met at the beginning of this chapter was a true witness, Langland's death was sudden but already welcome in his forethoughts. He had seen death's approach and asked Nature for what he called the 'vengeance' of deliverance and some parting words of advice.

> 'Counsel me, O Nature', he wrote, 'what craft is best to learn'.
> 'Learn to love', was the reply, 'and leave aside everything else'.
>   (B XX 207–8).

Chapter 2

LANDSCAPES AND PEOPLE

Piers Plowman sometimes gives the reader the sense that he is himself dreaming. Characters loom up and speak, and their words and actions generate emotion while the physical circumstances often, as in dreams, remain shadowy and vague.

What follows in this chapter and the next is an attempt to give Langland's world a physical, historical setting. That world is a part of England, not the whole, and we shall try to keep within the horizons which bounded Langland's own vision: the west Midlands and the swathe of country down to London and the south-east.

The student of literature may not feel a need for such explanations, but Langland cannot help being a historical source, and the historian may understand and enjoy what he wrote the better for a little history without forfeiting the poetry. Langland's poetic breath may stir the dead bones of his day.

The conventions of medieval poetry would sometimes have us believe it was always May-time, and even Langland with his selective care for detail leads us into his opening vision by way of a summer scene:

> In a somer seson, whan softe was the sonne,
> I shoop me into shroudes as I a sheep were . . .   (B Prol. 1–2)

> [I rigged myself out in rough clothes like a shepherd's]

Though conventional, there is an appropriateness about the opening image. For England was sheep country as well as corn country. To the south of Langland's Malvern lay the Cotswold hills and their great sheep-runs, where wool-merchants arrived every year to inspect and buy the finest fleeces. From Northleach at their heart the ride to London through the

Oxfordshire and Buckinghamshire countrysides took a man through both arable and pasture.

There is another reason besides the poem's opening image for beginning this discussion with sheep, and that is the special value of English wool in creating the wealth that perplexed Langland. *Piers Plowman* is admittedly agricultural in much of its dominant imagery, for the ancient basis of England's livelihood was the cultivated land. But her more recent and more extraordinary riches came from wool. If the day-labourers when they come on the scene seem routine characters at their dunging and ditching, the display and sophistication of the well-to-do derived more spectacularly from the manufacture and sale of woollen cloth.

Since the twelfth century at latest the kingdom had been growing richer as Italians, Flemings and then Englishmen exported wool and then cloth, and channelled into England a torrent of silver. Langland's young manhood witnessed the fortune-making of 'new' English families often, as it happened, from the eastern Midlands, like the de la Poles of Hull, who came to London and made their mark with their finance and their mode of speech. The age saw also the improving condition of many others in the wool and cloth industries: sheep-farmers with enormous flocks like the earls of Lancaster and many great abbeys down to quite modest folk whose wool the merchants also liked to buy; also the wool brokers, weavers, fullers and dyers. Wealth was generated in this manner and spent in hundreds of ways from great stone buildings to the pepper on sale in market towns and the little collections of books available to thrifty and educated people.

Langland, Chaucer and others refer to this activity indirectly. Perhaps the clothiers were especially close to Langland's world, since he was acutely conscious both of conspicuous wealth and also of changes in worldly fortune, and both wealth and change were very evident in what people wore.

Langland is always talking about appearances. In symbolic humility he 'roams about in russet', the cloth of peasants, country-made. As for Lady Meed, she was the scarlet woman herself:

> Hire robe was ful riche, of reed scarlet engreyned . . .   (B II 15)

which was to say that it was of the finest cloth, treated with the dye derived from kermes or cochineal insects, obtainable in the Near East and known in medieval records as 'grain'. Scarlet cloth dyed 'in the grain' (*in grano*) was reserved for the great, – kings and their judges and (since about 1300) the Roman cardinals; and however much the fourteenth century was an age of rising expectations, nobody below the highest ranks would have dared to appear so gorgeously dressed.

The English wool which supplied the looms of Flanders and Florence and increasingly of England herself enabled London with its rich companies of import-export merchants to stand as the only English city in the same bracket as the great urban centres of the Continent. Unlike much of the

Continent, the English countryside was also a land which enjoyed peace and prosperity. It might be argued that the wealth of England, regularly taxed by the king, made possible the long, wasteful wars against France. There is truth in this, but England was an island secure enough from alien kings and emperors, and her wealth also made possible a royal government which on the whole kept the peace and applied a common law. Langland was not basically a political thinker, as was argued in the Introduction, and he saw salvation much less in earthly rule than most other poets, but he could see the king as standing for justice and peace (he had Old Testament models too), and he could agree that wealth, even that of merchants, could be put to a right use. Langland was an apostle of moderation, not extremes, and his Englishness, often commented on, had an indirect link with the desirability of English wool.

From the sheep-runs, cloth-villages and wool-quays we turn to the agricultural scene. However well they were clothed, most English people were fed most of the time by English produce. What went into the cooking-pots of cottages and even of palaces was mostly grown, reared or caught in the fields, woods, rivers and shore-waters of home. Cereals were dominant, and the imagery of the poem comes more from the cornfield than from the flocks and herds appropriate to the psalmist in a more pastoral society. So although Langland prayed 'the Lord is my shepherd', his Christ was given the features of a ploughman. So too the common man personified among the rebels in 1381 was given the name in a popular refrain of 'Piers the ploughman', not of a shepherd who would have been too isolated a figure to strike chords of comradeship. From Langland himself we get more images of cultivation than of sheep-folding, clipping and the rest. We hear of oxen as the Evangelists, and read of harrow and sickle, and of the wide world at work upon one half-acre, naturally more peopled than the upland grazings.

The symbols are of great simplicity because the poet only needed to make readily available points. His episodes are often like parables. So the harrow was familiar to all as the great flat rake drawn by one or two work-horses ('stots') to break up and tear apart the clods to form tilth and disperse intruding weeds, and 'to harrow' was to destroy the weeds of vice amongst the seeds of virtue (C XXI 310–17). Even the sin of avarice was stylized in the action of ploughing in common fields, as Haukyn drove his team so craftily that he took in a foot or a furrow of his neighbour's strip, and at harvest-time got his reapers to lean over and sickle off corn he had not himself sown (B XIII 374).

These farming people produced the food of which Langland wrote so often, just as he did of rough and fine clothing, as signs of people's status.

The modern reader of *Piers Plowman* will, of course, be aware of crucial differences in the food-supply of the fourteenth century which give to his text the poignancy of ancient inequalities. They are inequalities mostly ironed out in the industrial west: of wealth, of bad harvests, and of the annual time-gap between the eating-up of available produce and the arrival of the next harvest.

First, there was the unbridgeable gap between rich and poor: Dives among the roasts in hall, Lazarus famished at the gate. There is no need in this context to dwell on the details of aristocratic eating save to point out its mixture of elaboration and grossness, and the uninterrupted availability of foodstuffs even in famine years.

Whether or not Langland was familiar himself with dining in a great hall, he conveys vividly the inequality of food-supply between rich and poor. There was plenty of money about in London and the cook-shops and taverns catered enticingly for those who could pay. 'Cooks and their servants cried "hot pies, hot! Good goose and pork! Come on in and dine!" Taverners too were shouting "white wine from Alsace, Gascon wine, wines from Rhineland and La Rochelle! Goes down well with the roast!"' (B Prol. 226–30).

London was special, both in *Piers Plowman* and in historical reality, as we shall see. But a high standard of living was quite possible to those with middling, regular incomes, even in the quietest corners of England. Such were the two priests and their servant who lived in Bridport, Dorset, and were spending about 40 pence a week on food and lighting in the 1450s. Money is impossible to translate into the figures of a totally different society, but the Bridport household seems to have been roughly at the standard of a skilled building worker at the time.[1] Though of the next generation to that of Langland, prices and wages had not greatly shifted, and on their income these unmarried gentlemen enjoyed an excellent mixed diet of fresh beef, lamb and pork, with goose and sucking-pig for a treat. Fish on days of abstinence included cod, hake, whiting, haddock and the ubiquitous herring, fresh or salted – and plenty of oysters. They did not consume great amounts of eggs, butter, milk or cheese, but got through a lot of oatmeal, local fresh fruit and vegetables, and a surprising variety of imported spices like pepper, cloves, ginger, cinnamon and saffron.

A description like this says little about general conditions, even without fluctuations, because we cannot know in detail how the poor managed nor in actuality how many were truly on breadline. Scholars who work away at average holdings and the notional possession of animals still have no historical evidence of calorie intake in the various households of fourteenth-century England.[2] Still, the Bridport household-

---

[1] K. L. Wood-Legh, *A small household of the fifteenth century* (Manchester, 1956). For medieval food-prices and wages, see E. H. Phelps-Brown and Sheila V. Hopkins, 'Seven Centuries of the prices of consumables, compared with builders' wage-rates', *Economica* (1956), reprinted in E. M. Carus-Wilson (ed.) *Essays in Economic History* (London, 1962), pp. 179–96.

[2] For a general but expert discussion see now Christopher Dyer, *Standards of living in the later Middle Ages* (Cambridge, 1989).

accounts provide a marker of what was possible to those in fairly fortunate circumstances.

A second kind of inequality which hit the poor majority hard came with the periodic bad harvest. The spectre of Hunger (*Fames*) was a familiar medieval motif, and Langland uses it effectively to preach a doctrine of honest work. To him a shortage of food was a moral matter, whether as a general punishment for sin or a particular consequence of avarice and sloth. It is easy to say he and all medieval people were ignorant of economic realities, but that is not wholly true. Scarcity and the movement of prices were recognized by merchants and those of intellectual training. But Langland had a different purpose in writing, and his text can convey something of the quality of life.

Again the actual details are inaccessible. We cannot know if it was common or rare to see people who had died of starvation. Literary descriptions suggest that plague was more spectacular. The severe European famine of 1315–17 just before Langland's time seems to have left many at starvation level, though probably not to the dramatically terrible extent of modern East Africa. In Langland's own lifetime there were periods of dearth during the 1350s and up to the 1370s, but accompanied by wage-rises to soften the impact for those in work, and there was a sharp fall in food prices from about 1370 which improved living-standards for many. *Piers Plowman* cannot be used as an economic indicator, but in the most general way conditions of near-famine along with unusual plenty for some people explain the poet's attitudes. His moralising dwells on the abrupt transitions from piteous hunger (mostly the fault of the hungry) to unseemly greed.

The text is also useful for its precise if anecdotal touches. In normal times the field-worker and even the beggar had his hunks of cheese and bacon (cf. C IX 147–50). In bad times the talk is of bread made with peas or beans, of beans and bran baked together, baked apples and any onions or greens the garden would yield (B VI 179–95), and for the poorest families most of the time coarse bread, thin ale, some cold meat or fish, and, on the fast days which they are represented as keeping, mussels or cockles could be a veritable feast (C IX 92–5).

The third inequality, hardly known in our society, was the relative scarcity of food in the weeks before harvest and its relative abundance when the harvest was gathered. In a famous passage Piers is made to exclaim to Hunger

> I have no peny . . . pulettes to bugge,
> Neither gees ne grys, but two grene cheses,
> A fewe cruddes and creme and a cake of otes,
> And two loves of benes and bran ybake for my fauntes.
> And yet I seye, by my soule, I have no salt bacon
> Ne no cokeney, by Crist, coloppes to maken!
> Ac I have percile and porettes and manye plaunte coles,

And ek a cow and a calf, and a cart mare
To drawe afeld my donge the while the droghte lasteth.
By this liflode we mote lyve till Lammesse tyme,
And by that I hope to have hervest in my crofte;
Thanne may I dighte thi dyner as me deere liketh.
(B VI 280–91)

[I haven't a penny to buy pullets nor goose or pork. All I've got is
a couple of fresh cheeses, a little curds and cream, an oat-cake
and two loaves of beans and bran baked for my children. And
upon my soul I haven't a scrap of bacon and, good God!, there's
no-one in the kitchen to fry meat – though I do have some parsley
and leeks and plenty of greens. Also I've got a cow and a calf, and
a mare to cart the manure during the dry weather. And with these
few things we must live till Lammas (1 August) when I hope to
get in the harvest of my croft. Then I'll put you on a dinner as I'd
really like to.]

When things got better, with new corn coming on to the market and the
people flush with harvest suppers or with money from their sales at market,
then Langland made the idlers and beggars demand fine white bread and the
darkest, strongest ale the brewsters could supply (B VI 304–6) and even the
landless labourers expected for their wages fresh meat or fish piping hot from
the oven –

And that *chaud* and *plus chaud*, for chillynge of hir mawe.
(B VI 311)

The final line, I think, is a stab of sarcasm from one who despite all his
compassion for the poor could never stomach the idea that those of low
degree should demand as of right the fare of their betters, which is to say
more than that he was merely disgusted with their gluttony; for his sentence
begins with the mocking French of the English gentleman and ends with the
gulping of beasts:

. . . and that's got to be *une assiette chaude* in front of their
frozen muzzles.

*   *   *

So far we have been looking at the landscape framework of life. The people
in the field, milling about in confusion, now need to be set in a perspective.
   Piers simply set them to work on his half-acre or, as we might say, a
notional strip of land, and a literal-minded reader might think this an
absurdly small patch. But the idea of crowding a number of people on to a
field is not as ridiculous as it might seem. In modern England with its

machine-cultivated sweeps of ploughland thick with heavy-headed corn, we can watch food appearing with hardly a human-being in sight.

But when Langland was young, England was coming to the end of a long period during which the population grew faster than the resources to support them. The upward curve seems to have faltered and turned only with the great famine of 1315–7 and then the plagues which became serious in 1348–9.

What had been happening for a couple of centuries was a busy ploughing up of new and often poorer land, and also the creation of many small plots and pieces either higgledy-piggeldy on the margins or even within the big common-fields. Of course a lot of the best English soil was kept in the possession of great lords and monasteries and worked for them both by serf and by paid labour. But an observer would not have to walk far from these so-called 'demesnes' to notice how much cultivated land was continually being divided up among tenants and sometimes joined up again in the hands of others. This was not just because of inheritances, but largely through buying, selling and leasing. Land was getting more valuable and there was a market for it. Some wanted to add acre to acre. Others needed to raise cash. Quite a lot of people desired to let out fields, pastures and even animals in order to make an income, perhaps for themselves and perhaps to pay for some family arrangement like having Masses said for the souls of kinsmen who had died.

In Langland's time this did not mean a great increase in the number of hedgerows. In open country local people used boundary markers which they were supposed to know but which were moveable or negotiable: standing stones, deeper furrows, water-courses and so on. A crafty man like Haukyn could ignore his neighbour's land-mark, but he must have been able to see it.

Not surprisingly, there was an enormous number of private land-transactions. With 'unfree' land these are just entries on the lord's parchment court-roll, but with the vast quantity of free land they survive as deeds or private 'charters' written in Latin, occasionally French, (rarely English till the fifteenth century) and recording the details of the deal. Thousands of these are in museums and archive offices and many in private hands. In the fourteenth century the stream of deeds became a flood, and the present writer has read many hundreds of them, of which two may be selected, almost at random, to show how ink can perpetuate the memory of ancient but precise property-deals.

In July 1322 Robert, the miller of Allexton near Uppingham (now in Leicestershire), bought three eighths of an acre as a single piece in one of the big fields of Belton called West Field. The piece lay between lands belonging to the chaplain of Belton and Ralph le Warde, and it was sold him by one Robert son of Emma. In September 1323, we are told by another parchment strip, the miller brought another lot comprising half an acre and quarter of an acre in other parts of the Belton fields. This time the seller was Robert le

Warde, and the portions were bounded by property of a William Cox, of a man called Nicholas le Freyne who was a tenant of one Peter Benet, and again of the chaplain.[3]

These two deeds show activity in the open countryside of the English Midlands on the morrow of an extremely severe famine. A local miller was buying, and a man like that was usually prosperous, almost a village capitalist. If we wonder incidentally why the miller of Dee in the old song was both jolly and unloved we might have an answer in his possession of local milling monopoly, possibly his local money-lending, and his ability, as here, to lay acre to acre.

There is a further point. The huge number of people who were buying, selling and leasing property by the fourteenth century were not all agriculturalists. Some acquired plots or buildings to carry on a trade in village or town, some to set up shops or shambles (as for instance in Sevenoaks market-place), some to get a dwelling-house. Chaucer had a place in the sought-after East Greenwich area; Langland's father was a tenant of Lord Spencer. Nobles were not the only landlords. Prosperous people like merchants could invest in house-property just as well as in fields or workshops.

It will be obvious that to think of Langland's England as simply a society of 'lords and peasants' is a great over-simplification. At one extreme were the London-dwellers, to be met at the end of this chapter. But in village England a wide variety of people lived side by side. A minority of farming families were comparatively rich in their possession of one, two or even more hundred acres of good land, and were able to employ others both to cultivate this and if necessary to perform any services they might owe to lords above them in a legal or tenurial way. Below this village aristocracy (who could be 'franklins', or unpolished 'yeomen', or even men hoping to conceal their unfree origins) came others of modest means, possessing between, say, fifteen and a hundred acres. Probably half the population were of this sort, and their prosperity varied greatly, according to the quality as well as the amount of their land and many other unknowable circumstances like health, personality, size of family, other enterprises and so on.

At the bottom were the poor, families trying to live off very few acres or only a cottage and a garden, or even off nothing but the support of kinsmen, if any, and what they might earn from farm labour. Cripples and handicapped people were a common sight if the literature is to be believed, and there were widows living alone and also, one may suppose from church-court records, unmarried women with or without children. These people are invisible to statistics but vivid to a gifted poet. One of Langland's best-known passages – 'the most needy are our neighbours' (C IX 70–87) – paints a picture of a cottager family.

---

[3] Original deed in private hands; transcript with present author.

Before the plagues England was an overpopulated country in the sense that there was often neither sufficient food or work for everybody. More people would have been apparent in the village fields than today, picking up what jobs they could find, gleaning or loafing about for lack of work. Loss of population through epidemics, as we shall see, made some difference; but the crowded and assorted nature of Piers's half-acre is a literary device with historical sense behind it.

It is also clear that we cannot usefully speak simply about 'peasants'. At best it is a vague word. In reality the group of men clustered round a heavy plough were probably much different from each other. The boss might be its actual owner – even men of some social standing sometimes rolled up their sleeves – or he might be working for a distant lord or master. His helpers might be sons, or employees whom he paid and who might themselves hardly own a sickle. This is why 'Piers the ploughman' is such a generalized figure.

But in any case a heavy plough drawn by oxen and/or horses was valuable, and it needed both skill and authority to use it successfully day in day out, turning at the headlands and getting the maximum out of the beasts but keeping them in good shape. It needed a little team of people to drive it, and the overseer, whom we might well call the 'ploughman' was sometimes styled in the Latin as *dominus caruce*, 'the lord of the plough'. The others are often called the boys or servants (*garciones, famuli*).[4] In the poem itself Piers is at this point a man who hired his own helpers on his own land, hence more of a 'peasant' figure than either a lord or a lord's bondman. He certainly had the power to hire and fire like the householder in the Gospel who engaged day-labourers for his vineyard (Mt. 20):

> At high prime Piers let the plough stand
> To oversee himself who worked best
> And who should be hired thereafter . . .   (B VI 112–4)

It is only too easy to write of the middle ages as though they formed a long period when nothing changed, when people moved little either socially or geographically and the world was oppressive and benighted by comparison with what was to come. But the more one thinks about the fourteenth century the less it seems to belong to a mythical 'dark age' and the closer its style to the more modern world. Between 1300 and 1400 serfdom was ceasing to be a dominant condition in village life, the land market was active, people moved about more in getting their living, the English language was becoming more standardized, while the social classes into which people divided themselves were adopting English names – particularly 'gentleman' – through the usage of those anxious to assert their social as well as legal status.

[4] F. R. H. Du Boulay, *The Lordship of Canterbury* (1966), p. 171.

In looking at this changing society it is easier to start from the bottom. This means talking about unfreedom, not about poverty. Though allied they were not the same. Serfdom, bondage, villeinage, call it what you will, was still alive in Langland's day, and the abolition of unfreedom was one of the demands of the rebels of 1381.

No doubt most serf families were poor, and many of the poor were serfs. But a man with only a cottage might be personally free, while a bondman might with luck and work become quite affluent.

The scales were weighted against the unfree. A bondman usually had more and heavier rents to pay, and probably owed various labour services to a lord in respect of his holding. He was also liable to quite humiliating conditions on account of his servile status, such as payments on the occasions of his father's death and his daughters' marriages. There is evidence that the stigma of bondage was felt even when actual services or payments were light. We do not need to be told today that people feel their social status just as keenly as their wealth or poverty.

There was no sudden emancipation of the serfs. Some prospered and were able to buy their freedom. This was called 'manumission', and was done under the fiction of a loan of money from the lord, as a bondman in legal theory could not own his own wealth.

A more usual way – though it is unprovable – was probably the silent prospering of serf families which could afford to get the labour services they owed performed for them by poorer neighbours in return for payment, so that in the course of time the personal debt of service could get forgotten altogether. This is suggested by case where it did *not* happen because a lord woke up and made a fuss. There is a fifteenth-century letter written from Blackham in Sussex to the prior of Canterbury, a great lord whose monastery (Canterbury Cathedral) had some land there.[5] The prior's agent reported, 'there are bondmen here belonging to your manor, and they are rich men'. The informer, doing his job, went on to say that 'if it please your lordship to search in your treasury among your old court rolls, you may find names like those of these men, and you may be able to get 100 marks [£66.66p], for it is said "whatever the serf acquires is acquired for his lord".' Of course the agent meant that these unfortunates would be glad to pay a good sum to be made free.

This was a little later than Langland's time, but it shows that serfdom was disappearing slowly. In Langland's lifetime it was still very much alive. The ancient contradiction had not yet been resolved. From St Paul right through the middle ages the message ran that in Christ there was neither bond nor free, yet also that in this sinful world the unfree and the subject should obey their worldly masters.

The Anglo-Saxon King Ethelred (978–1016) had thought it very wrong

[5] J. Brigstocke Sheppard (ed.), *Christ Church Letters* (Camden New Series 19, 1877), No. lxxx.

that innocent Christians should be enslaved, while the archbishop of Canterbury as late as 1361 refused to emancipate a young man at Uckfield in Sussex when he sold their freedom to the youngster's brothers.[6]

Langland's own views were what we might expect: compassionate yet tough; unworldly but schematically theological. He wrote constantly with deep pity for the poor, even when they brought suffering upon themselves. He hated the personal arrogance of rich to poor. Yet he regarded serfdom as a consequence of original sin, and said that the villein could not escape his bondage by running away (as a lot did), any more than a baptized person could renounced his Christianity:

> For may no cherl chartre make ne his chatel sulle
> Withouten leue of the lord . . .   (C XII 60f.)

> [No serf may execute a deed or sell his property without his lord's leave.]

At the same time Langland thought that Christ's death on the cross enacted a gigantic manumission for all who believed in him and that the serf was in this way a blood-brother of every other Christian (B XI 199–203; C XII 107–110). In fact it was wise not to injure your underlings whom you might quite well see one day at a heavenly top-table.

Langland's theory had a disagreeable side also in blaming the disabilities of the Jews on their rejection of Jesus. Once, he said, the Jews were *gentel men*, but then they became *lowe cherles* who all over the world lived under tribute and tallage as *tykes and cherles*. Those who had become Christian by following the advice of John the Baptist were 'franklins and free men and gentle men with Jesus'. Langland equated Christ's family with his own in the freedom they shared and of which he was deeply proud. To Langland Christ's mother was a *gentil womman* though betrothed to a poor man, and Christ himself was not born in a beggar's cottagé but, though in an out-house, in 'a burgeises place' (B XI 246–7; XII 148).

History did not wait for Langland. Those he saw at the base of the divinely-ordered pyramid were not staying there, and the world was being upset and changed by catastrophes which he would ascribe to sin yet brought betterment to many English people. For one thing the Jews whose faithlessness he deplored had been expelled from England in 1290, long before his own birth, and were even as he wrote improving the fortunes of their lords and themselves in the finance-departments of Rhineland princes like the duke of Cleves and the prince-archbishop of Trier. In England itself social changes of great importance were coming about largely through the reduction of population by human and animal disease.

---

[6] Register of Archbishop Simon Islip (Lambeth Palace Library), fos. 151v–152; also J. Brigstocke Sheppard (ed.), *Literae Cantuarienses* (Rolls Series 85, 1887–9), vol. ii, No. 880.

It is a familiar story which may be told fairly quickly. High mortality altered English life without disrupting it. The most important development was the rise in wages brought about by the shortage of labour.

The first great visitation of the plague petered out in the summer of 1349, and the same year Edward III made an order to freeze wages. In 1351 the king's parliament confirmed this by the first Statute of Labourers, which spoke in alarm of 'the malice of servants who [are] idle and not willing to serve after the pestilence without excessive wages'.[7] Particular examples may be drawn from all parts of the country, but this chapter may be suitably illustrated from Chelmsford in Essex and Shrewsbury in Shropshire, neither of them very far from regions Langland would have known.

In 1352 some ploughmen at Chelmsford were accused before the royal judges of asking 18 to 20 pence an acre instead of the previous hire-price of 10 pence or less for their services.[8] In 1354 the bishop of Coventry and Lichfield noted the ruinous state of some monastic buildings at Shrewsbury, but wrote to the monks, 'this is not through your fault but through the malice of the times and the rarity of workmen'.[9] Whatever the reputation of ploughmen as ideal figures, they were no more immune than others from the laws of supply and demand. But the age explained these in moral terms. The 'malice' of labourers is echoed by the 'malice' of the times, and to Langland who was living through the effects there was no doubt such calamities came from sin.

Plague had the power to make a terrible impression because it was less a respecter of persons than famine. The well-to-do could buy food at enormous prices or command it from their estates. Disease was different. Some were able to flee infected places but were still struck down. 'Nature coming out of the planets sent out his foragers: fever and fluxes . . . cramps . . . and burning agues' (B XX 80ff.).

Outlining the course of this first plague, the statute made clear it was mainly unskilled or semi-skilled manual workers who refused to work at less than double or treble the previous rates, and it named specifically 'carters, ploughmen, drivers of the plough, shepherds, swineherds, day labourers . . . threshers . . . carpenters, masons, tilers and other workers on houses . . . thatchers with fern and straw, plasterers and other workers on mud walls'. These plain words are useful in constructing a mental picture of field, village and town.

All these men were said to be infected with the spirit of 'covetousness'. Secular and church laws as well as poetry made play with this concept of avarice. 'Their ease and singular covetousness', rang the statute, and at the

---

[7] Alec R. Myers (ed.), *English Historical Documents, 1327–1485* (1969), p. 993.

[8] B. H. Putnam, *The Enforcement of the Statute of Labourers* (New York, 1908), p. 405.

[9] Ex inf. N. F. Swanson, University of Birmingham, 1986.

same time the archbishop of Canterbury was forbidding the clergy subject to his jurisdiction to ask for higher stipends, and his law was known from its opening words as 'Unbridled covetousness' (*Effrenata cupiditas*). The same word is used many times in *Piers Plowman*, where the working-man's greed was a dominant theme: 'if he be not hired for high wages he will curse' (B VI 312).

Of course medieval men believed readily in a mysterious right-ness called a 'just price', said to be easily agreed as reasonable; and Conscience was made to lecture the king that money which labourers take from their masters does not count as filthy lucre (Meed) at all, but is a 'measurable hire' or appropriate wage (B III 256); but it is noticeable that this comment got left out of the last version of the poem.

Whatever kings and moralists might say, the Statutes of Labourers were only partially and temporarily effective. For one thing, the local justices who were supposed to enforce it had a personal interest in hiring labour on their own farms, and they could put up their prices a bit to pay the going rate.

The dilemma did not last for ever. In the 1370s, after a couple more severe epidemics, the demand for corn became less than the supply and the price tumbled. It was evidently from that point that landlords really felt the need to apply the wage-pegging statutes. The 1370s was a restive decade when important landlords began to lease off fields at what price they could get, and when labourers became angry both at wage-fixing and at the attempts to insist on old servile customs which demanded they do work for little or nothing. The Great Revolt of 1381 was triggered off by poll-taxes which bore on the poor rather than the rich, but the way had been prepared for the explosion by the harsh actions of landlords – the men of Bench and Parliament – who thought it both desirable and right to keep up the old ways.

The Revolt was crushed and did not recur: wages found their own level and life was not made intolerable for the labouring population. This was in the future and outside our present theme. Of course people at the time were terribly frightened, and in 1388 an even more severe Statute of Labourers was enacted[10] which Langland might well have approved if he were still alive, as it showed a great fear of beggars and vagrants, some of whom were said to join pilgrimages to pursue their begging, and who were anyhow hard to distinguish from men moving about the country looking for work at high wages.

Many themes of *Piers Plowman* are explicable in the light of these changes. There was not only the obsession with beggars, especially mobile ones, but also the disapproval throughout the poem of clothing and personal belongings which were both expensive and apparently unsuitable for the classes of person now able to afford them. Parliament itself was already in 1363 legislating against 'outrageous and excessive apparel' and trying to

[10] *EHD* as in Note 6 above, pp. 1002–4.

make ploughmen, shepherds and their like wear only cheap clothing made of blanket or russet.[11]

This was the world which Langland thought could be improved by stern husbands calling to order their wives for buying extravagant hats, and fathers spanking their children. He saw with uncanny accuracy that the plague was connected with available money to spend on the children who would anyhow be the more treasured because they had been spared:

> Let no profit weaken them while they are young, and do not
> for the power of the pestilence please them out of reason.
>
> (B V 35–6)

The confession of the Seven Deadly Sins (B V) is very much a document of the late fourteenth century.

But neither the changes in English society nor the themes of *Piers Plowman* were limited to the labouring population. Moving up the social ladder we come to the lesser commercial classes and also to the so-called gentry.

Right at the poem's beginning we noticed that those who lived by trade were among the many groups who were always moving about. Though impossible to measure, it is hard to avoid the impression that Langland's England was becoming a very mobile society. There is an old but deservedly famous book called *English Wayfaring Life in the Middle Ages* written by a Frenchman called J. J. Jusserand. He illustrated some of the travellers on England's medieval roads: rich ladies in carts, waggons of hay, squires, messengers, pilgrims and so forth. It is still worth reading, though we now realize that travel was incessant for many more kinds of people. Even the poor might go considerable distances in the service of others, or to escape unemployment, a bad local reputation or even an unhappy marriage. With those who were not so poor, travel was often part of getting a living, for instance by transferring money or goods from one place to another. A couple of examples will make the point. Even though they come from the fifteenth century their circumstances reach back to the England Langland knew.

The records of Southampton disclose that merchandise of many sorts passing through the port was distributed far and wide by carting businesses like that of the Hekles [= Hickley]. With their three carts they took stuff inland as far as Coventry in the Midlands, charging one penny per ton-mile, and their annual profit was somewhere round £50 – better than that of many sheep-owners or skilled building workmen.[12]

Doing business at a distance is also shown by the problem of two sisters

---

[11] Stat. 37 Edward III c. 14.

[12] Olive Coleman, 'Trade and Prosperity in fifteenth-century Southampton . . .' *Economic History Review* 2nd series XXVI No. 1 (August 1963), pp. 9–22.

called Alice and Joan Preston. Living in Stanwell, near Heathrow, they came into some property in the Isle of Wight from their father and in their affluence moved to London. Here they discovered the need for a lawyer, like many in their position, so they appointed a Citizen called John Taylor as their attorney to take possession of the Isle of Wight property and do all the business in connection with letting it.[13] Today a few signatures would be sufficient authority. In August 1427, the date of this business, however, the proper authentication was the impress of an identifiable seal, and the sisters were cautious enough to realize that the seals of the many little-known people like themselves were not convincing enough. So they had a clause added to their attorney's letter which read, 'and because the seals of Alice and Joan are unknown to very many people, they have sealed the present instrument with the seal of Robert Tatershal, an alderman of London'.

Tatershal was a rich Draper with a place in Essex;[14] his daughter married a knight and his son was later called 'gentleman', and this brings us to the next layer of society in this discussion of Langland's changing England.

Historians used to write as though some particular age saw in England a 'rise of the gentry' as a class of political and social importance. Whatever may be true of Tudor or Stuart England, the phrase is not really appropriate to the fourteenth century, despite the great changes which were undoubtedly occurring.

Politically England was an aristocratic society, and politics were still in the fifteenth century a matter for 'lords'. Socially England had long possessed a class of moderately well-off landholders who took the lead in local affairs and even sent representatives at the king's command to his parliaments. Successful merchants could also belong to this rather shapeless society below noble rank. But it is too early in date to use the abstract word 'gentry'.

In Langland's world the most noticeable changes were from a dominant French to a dominant English, and a rise and fall of individuals in the social scale which was the subject of comment.

Langland and Chaucer wrote of *gentil men* though the English word does not become common till the fifteenth century. If an abstract noun was wanted it was likely to be *gentilesse*, not the English 'gentry', and gentilesse referred to personal qualities like manners and up-bringing. They were status words applicable to individuals, used because a term was needed in a fluid society without rigid, heritable caste-titles.

It is interesting that Langland himself is likely to be talking about coming down in the world when he uses this vocabulary. Mary, mother of Jesus, was a *gentel womman* even though a truly poor maiden wedded to a poor man (B XI 246–7). The Jews before their refusal to recognize the Messiah had been *gentel men* but had become *cherles* (C XXI 34–5). In his own day Langland

---

[13] Original deed in private hands.
[14] Sylvia Thrupp, *The Merchant Class of Medieval London* (1948), p. 369.

remarked bitterly how knighthoods went for money while popes and patrons gave church livings for money and *pore gentel blood refused* (C V 78). In fact he did not find it easy to separate the idea of deference to holiness from that of deference to social position. Perhaps he found it hard to curb a personal resentment. Elsewhere he was able to forget an unfair world and see that knights looked no different from knaves in the graveyard (B VI 49), remembering his psalter

> Ordinary people are a mere puff of wind, important men a
>   delusion   (Ps. 62:9)

The writer of *Piers Plowman* had a special concern for the poor, a sharp eye to observe and a heart to pity. But he lived in a world ruled by 'lords' which would be entirely familiar to him and his audience, so modern readers of his text may find a short discussion of the lords of England helpful.

At the outset we are entitled to doubt how familiar Langland was with lordly households. Many of his comments on them are critical and sharp, and since the rich do not often enjoy paying for entertainment they dislike nor, any more than the rest of us, hasten to encourage public reproof, it may well be that the households Langland reports as welcoming were those of unpretentious people and no doubt devout ones at that.

'Lord' is quite a general word. The Anglo-Saxon root-word, *hlaford*, was the 'loaf-keeper', the provider for his followers, which gives in some ways a better perspective on English noblemen than do the Latin *dominus* or the French *seigneur*.

But by the fourteenth century both 'lord' and 'dominus' could be used in all kinds of contexts. There was the 'lord king', and there were the 'lords' whom the king summoned individually to his parliaments (which was what in England actually made them lords). But you could also use it simply as a respectful form of address to a man who was, say, a graduate in theology or some sort of estate owner, not a nobleman at all.

Langland used it in various connections. One is when he writes about the envious man who does his luckier neighbour a bad turn by slandering him to important people, and makes him say, 'I have often made his life a misery and told lies against him to lords' (B V 93). The point is merely about telling damaging tales to social superiors, and its interest is principally in describing a society, however aristocratic it was, that gave opportunities like most other societies for unimportant household servants to gossip familiarly with their masters.

But 'lords' very often refers to landholders, great and small, and this is what non-specialists usually mean when they talk about medieval 'lords'.

Very generally, a lord was anyone who possessed a court to which his tenants had to come. Little manorial courts met every three weeks in a room, hall or even open air under the lord's steward or bailiff. Their business was the regulation of local custom about the succession to unfree land and the payment of dues. They looked after work on fields and small matters of social behaviour, and in doing so yielded the lord a modest addition to his income and gave his lordship a public face. More important lords could also have courts of minor jurisdiction which met half-yearly. So the medieval lord had some of the characteristics of a magistrate over his own tenants as well as manager and registrar.

The lord was also a possessor of property, and this could be the rents he got from tenants or the produce he derived from the land cultivated especially and directly for him, called his 'demesne land'. He could of course have both demesne and also tenant land. If he were the rector of a church he would also have the right to a tithe of his parishioners' corn and produce. The tithe-barn in its way was also a symbol of lordship.

It goes without saying that lords needed labourers. Free or unfree, the small number of permanent workers were usually paid something and also had their own plots. A much larger proportion of the community were needed at harvest, and they too gave their labour according to local custom, usually for a combination of money and food and drink. Labour requires supervisors and watchmen, and when the poet wrote how he was interrogated by Reason about his livelihood, some of the questions were

> Can you reap and have you been a reap-reeve [foreman] and got up early? Have you taken a horn as hayward, and lain out at nights And kept my corn in my croft from pickers and thieves?   (C V 15–17)

The lordship of a great nobleman differed in degree rather than kind from that of the rural gentleman. It might extend over several shires and comprise woods, pastures and waste land as well as arable, meadow, fisheries and village communities of tenants. Lordship of someone from king downwards extended over all the land – country and town – often in ways so intermingled with each other that map-makers are baffled.

A special word is needed about church lordship. Much of the best land in England had come by gift and purchase into the possession of bishoprics and monasteries. By Langland's time there were other ecclesiastical lords of lands and tenants like Oxford colleges and privately endowed chantries. There were also corporate lordships of a secular kind like city gilds and companies.

The big Benedictine abbeys became rather especially unpopular as land-lords at this time for being hard landlords (and efficient ones). Langland spent relatively little space on criticizing monks, but raised sharp objections to those who emerged from their monasteries to act as their own stewards and in doing so displayed the personal arrogance he so hated:

> Now is Religion a rider, a roamer by streets,
> Presider at courts and buyer of land,
> Riding on palfreys from manor to manor
> With hounds at his arse as if he were a lord,
> And if his man doesn't kneel when he hands him a cup
> He glares at the fellow and asks who taught him manners.
>
> (from B X 303–8)

Since on the other hand Langland was obsessed with bitterness about the friars – a subject for later chapters – it should be said here that one of the original ideas of the friars was to avoid having any lordship over lands and tenants; and whatever their faults they kept pretty exactly to that rule. The wealth of fourteenth-century friars was wholly different, since it derived not from remote acres but from great popularity with people in centres of population and resulted in buildings with fine contents and churches rather than the sort of lordship discussed in this chapter.

We cannot understand medieval society unless we also realize that it was organized in households. The king himself ruled the estate that was his kingdom from his household. During the middle ages some parts of this great household became in effect formal business offices. For instance the Exchequer was a glorified version of the Checker in which every big monastery kept track of its credits and debts: the name comes from the striped cloth on which calculations were done with counters – ancestor of computers.

But the idea of government from offices which are shut up at night when secretaries go home to their families developed only slowly. The king's household was the centre of politics, and his will was carried out from that household, wherever it might be. If he were in Westminster or London it was easy to translate the royal commands into written form, through the ancient departments of Chancery or Exchequer, or through the Wardrobe or, less formally, through the clerks and knights who staffed his Chamber. But often the king was not at a fixed place of government but away hunting, campaigning or showing himself elsewhere in his realm. But he still ruled personally and could normally send his written or spoken orders to any of his innumerable officers to be carried out. When in *Piers Plowman* (B IV 193–4) the king promised to rule by the counsel of Conscience his words had a doubly direct meaning, for medieval rule was personal rule and, although ideally guided by the loyal counsel of others, the Conscience was by definition the king's.

Lords had smaller-scale replicas of a royal household, and even a prosperous knight could expect to dine in his hall, pray in his oratory, and talk about his accounts in a private chamber.

It was not a very private life, and in fact the love of domestic privacy most of us feel today was only emerging slowly in the fourteenth century. William Langland was rather interesting about this, for he complained that the Hall became a sorry, deserted place when the lord and the lady would not sit there every day. He declared that rich people were preferring to eat by themselves in a private room with its own fireplace (B X 96ff.). Sardonically, he supposed they were out to save money but cutting down on the amount of food cooked which could then be distributed as left-overs to the poor. But if Langland had been personally rebuffed and turned away from a hall, his words may be alluding to this and suggesting that important people had not liked the earnest tone of the entertainment he would offer them (C XI 31–4), for he goes on to comment on affluent lay people who liked to talk doubtful theology over their wine with fashionable clerics: 'drivelling on the dais in discussing the Deity' (C XI 40).

In an age when people made their own entertainment either by conversation or inviting professionals to perform or recite, the dinner-table was a centre of relaxation, and one of Langland's special resentments was the misuse of these social hours by crude displays or, much worse, by pseudo-intellectual and mocking discussions on subjects like the Trinity or original sin.

All the same, the life of big households continued to revolve round communal dinner in hall where family, guests and hangers-on were present. We cannot know exactly how the food was distributed, but on ordinary days wine was probably served to guests of quality, ale to the rest. Much more important was the position assigned to you in hall, as it has continued to be from Scriptural times to the present. Arguing that the great thing was to get to heaven and never mind where you sat, Imaginatif is made to say that a rich man might give a lowly fellow plenty of good food and put him to eat in the middle of the floor, where he would be with the company but without as much honour 'as those who sit at a side-table or with the sovereigns of the hall' (B XII 200).

A great lord who sat at his high table and glanced round his household gathered about him would be able to see all his own attendants, retainers and servants wearing his livery. This is an important word. Nowadays it is hardly used except to describe the uniform of a chauffeur or commissionaire. But it is a direct rendering of the Latin *liberatio* or 'delivery', in the sense of the standard issue at regular intervals of what a contracted retainer was owed by agreement with his lord. In a large household everyone, squires, gentlemen, grooms, pages, had fixed rations which included not only bread, drink and candles for their own quarters but also appropriate clothing in the same identifiable colours but of different quality according to rank. A court gentleman, for example, would get twice a year 'delivery of robes of the suit of gentlemen' (*liberatio robarum de secta generosorum*) as part of his payment. This is what Langland meant when he said through the mouth of Scripture that God is often met among needy people, whereas you do not see him much *in secte of the riche* (B XI 242–3).

So lords in their households lived among dependents and servants who were clothed and fed according to their grades, and would expect to be on more or less familiar terms with their lord. Some in a large household would be young people from 'good' families receiving training in courteous and courtly behaviour. It was a world where father and mother could be more remote figures than one's own 'good lord' under whose patronage one learned how a household ran, from the making of beds to the singing of a song.

This was only the apex of organized lordship. The wealth so conspicuously distributed from Kitchen and Wardrobe was produced and collected from the lord's estates or bought at markets and fairs or even, in the luxury class, ordered personally from a rich import-merchant.

Estates were run by councils composed partly of men of rank like knights who had local knowledge and influence, and partly of professional stewards, lawyers, auditors and clerks of accounts. Such men were well-paid office-holders who earned their living by long hours in the saddle, inspecting, interviewing, perhaps holding a court, and writing up the records on parchment rolls. Money had to be collected and safely transported in bags on horseback to the lord's household or some other treasury. There were also many bills, receipts, obligations and other documents. Management in the fourteenth century was already a profession, often but by no means always carried out by clerics. Basic skills were taught at a few schools like the one held by Thomas Sampson in Oxford[15] – not part of the university. But mostly young men learned on the job and if lucky got promoted and even retained to serve more than one estate. Again we catch Langland's disapproving eye as at the confession of Sloth he makes the old priest admit that he cannot sing or read saints' lives but knows how to put up a hare, preside at settlement-days and hear a reeve's reckoning (B V 416–21).

* * *

At an unknown time in the middle of the fourteenth century William Langland came to work in London and the surrounding country. We have to believe this not just because he wrote

And so y leue yn London and opelond bothe (C V 44)

[and so I live both in London and in the country]

but because the London detail in the poem is copious and circumstantial enough to carry conviction. Yet vivid as the scenes are where they involve persons, the scenery itself is maddeningly imprecise. This was in the nature of the poet whose dialogues and descriptions of figures and gestures are at the forefront of his impact but his interest in precise details of place rather vague.

[15] H. G. Richardson, 'Business Training in medieval Oxford', *American Historical Review*, vol. 46 (1941), pp. 259–80.

No modern writer can improve Langland, but putting him in a topo-
graphical frame may possibly show him off better.

The largest city in the realm had become a capital. This was partly because
it contained the kingdom's greatest concentration of merchants, but mainly
because it lay, joined by the thoroughfare known as the Strand, close by the
permanent quarters of the royal government at Westminster. These two
great settlements needed each other, the one spreading royal protection and
privilege upon the business-place of the rich, the other at hand to supply
money as gift, loan and tax, as well as fine provisions and beautiful treasures
for the king. A contemporary source described London as 'the king's
chamber and a mirror to all England'.

Westminster was not just a soulless administrative capital. Its ancient
abbey was very specially the king's church, where he was crowned and where
the crown jewels were kept. The abbey was dedicated to St Edward the
Confessor to whom Henry III had had a great devotion. Relics of the earlier
kings of the English were kept there and were even more sacred objects than
the regalia of crown, sceptre and orb. The great feast day was 13 October,
and this was a time when the king often stayed in his Palace at Westminster.

Not surprisingly, Westminster was a favourite location for royal councils
and parliaments and a natural site for permanent departments of finance and
law, so that important office-holders would need accommodation there.
When in the fourteenth century the Commons habitually attended parliament they too needed accommodation. Such people sometimes had business
of their own to attend to in Westminster and London. In addition again, the
clergy had taken to holding their own meeting at the request of the king:
Convocation of Canterbury spent a lot of its time discussing the clergy's
taxes, and they often met in Blackfriars where there was enough space and
good access by river.

In short, London-Westminster was a centre to which the power, wealth,
talent and business of the kingdom crowded. Westminster, the Strand and
parts of the City were thick with the palaces and inns (i.e. dwelling-houses)
of the great. Every great man had his retinue of servants, whether he was an
earl from the country, a bishop or a business-speculator like Richard Lyons
with his new fortune invested partly in house-property. The thought of
retinues in their liveries trying to clear a way for their masters conjures up
the hubbub. Brawls broke out easily, not seldom stimulated by ale and wine.
Back in the twelfth century the London writer FitzStephen had already
observed how his beloved city was often disfigured by 'the immoderate
drinking of fools'.

We cannot know how Langland first approached London, but whichever
way he went it was by a road through fields and villages now solid in brick and
concrete. Today we are accustomed to find many of the more prosperous
people living in well-to-do suburbs, miles from their places of week-day

work, while tracts of inner city lie decayed and inhabited by the poorest. In the middle ages it was generally the other way round. But medieval suburbs must be thought of in a different way, for they clustered and spilled over near the surrounding city wall and its rubbish-filled ditch outside.

London itself was extending a bit in the fourteenth century outside the wall, especially towards Holborn, and also south of the river in Southwark. But to approach on horse or foot from any direction was to pass through villages like Hoxton or Islington and to see green fields until you came by the causeway over the marshy ground outside the wall itself.

Naturally the surrounding settlements had connections of one kind or another with London's life, and if we accept Langland's phrase about getting a living both in London and the country (upland) it is likely that it was among these nearer and well-inhabited parts that he made his monthly rounds. Tottenham, for example, was beginning to turn into a cattle area for the London butchers who drove their beasts in for slaughter and for sale in East or West Cheap or at St Nicholas Shambles near Newgate.[16] Four or five miles north-east of the city, Stratford baked a lot of bread for the working population, to whom people like Haukyn brought it by cart early in the morning (B XIII 265–7), though clearly many people got baking done in the city itself from corn sold there.

The River Thames was the artery of supply, crowded with boats from the Continent and also from the coal and corn ports on England's east coast, and round from Woolwich and Erith loaded with timber and firewood for shipwrights, coopers and brewers.

Southwark on the south bank, connected with the City by London Bridge, was a vulnerable quarter. It was not only on the road to Canterbury and the coast which men of peace would take, but coming the other way it was a supply-line attractive to robbers and the obvious line of march for hostile armies and rebels. In the midst were large religious houses, St Mary Overie (Southwark Cathedral now) and Bermondsey Priory; also brothels where the girls were sometimes known as 'Winchester geese' after the great local landlord.

Moving a little up-river on the south bank one came to the turn the Saxons called *cearring*: over the water was Charing Cross, and a little further up still on the south bank was the archbishop of Canterbury's palace of Lambeth. From here it was a short row over to Westminster, passing within sight of the archbishop's low-lying fields at Lambeth Wick where his cattle were fattened for his hall dinners. Where today's clergy and scholars pass unobtrusively through the Palace gates, Langland's contemporaries were able to walk, as did Margery Kemp a few years later, to hear 'the archbishop's

---

16 Douglas Moss, 'The economic development of a Middlesex village', *Agricultural History Review*, vol. 28 (1980), pp. 104–114.

clerks, and other reckless men, both squires and yeomen', swearing and shouting.[17]

The City would have been seen better from the high ground to its north than from Thameside. It was a townscape of towers and tiled roofs behind the encircling wall. The two miles of wall from Blackfriars in the west stretched round in a rough semicircle to the Tower of London in the east, and they were punctuated in the fourteenth century by eight gates which were closed and guarded at night. The gates themselves were built up in order to provide accommodation, like that which Chaucer enjoyed for a time from 1374 in Aldgate. Newgate and Ludgate were jails.

Fourteenth-century London obeyed no overall plan but lay pell-mell as the product of innumerable decisions to found and build. Narrow thoroughfares pressed through the City as if against an ever-threatening wave of encroaching structures. Dominated by St Paul's cathedral and a number of great religious houses, the ecclesiastical atmosphere was carried from highway into lane by the hundred or so parish churches which were set among a vast number of tiny taverns and brew-houses jostling among dwellings and shops.

If Langland lived as he said in a Cornhill cottage, his home lay on a narrow east-west street in the middle of a city of lanes, where walkers passed countless dark doors from which could puff the fumes of ale, candle-wax and incense, and the stench of lock-ups.

Piers Plowman was about a world of inequalities – about fine lords, parsons and merchants in fur who walked with attendants past hovels of the poor and cells, or 'pits', where prisoners sat in fetters. Langland's skill lay not least in portraying a tense co-existence of rich and poor, stirred into periodic uproar but not yet shaped by any real political ideology.

The vivid account of the Great Revolt of 1381 in London offered by the so-called *Anonimalle Chronicle*[18] gives a sense of confusion. Common people in crowds surge in from north and south, welling up at Southwark until the bridge was let down and they flowed across shouting. The writer was interested in the damage done and noted the beating down of many houses and the firing of some. But when he tells us that the rebels came through Fleet Street, breaking open the prison and setting alight the shops of a chandler and a blacksmith 'in the middle of the street' and then tearing off the tiles of a house at the Temple so that the buildings were without any roofing, then we begin to see that even this crowd out of control was not destroying the city. Certainly the hatred was directed towards the power of law and money, but the city was not engulfed as in the Great Fire of 1666,

---

[17] W. Butler-Bowden (ed.), *The Book of Margery Kempe: a modern version* (Oxford: the World's Classics, 1954), p. 47.

[18] V. H. Galbraith (ed.), *The Anonimalle Chronicle*, excerpt reprinted in *EHD*, as in Note 7 above, pp. 27–40.

and though no less combustible it had a sturdiness of tile and stone created by a wealth hitherto unexampled in England.

In the City of London only about one-third of some forty thousand people belonged to citizen families. The rest, by and large the poor, were 'foreigns' except for an appreciable number of those we ourselves would call foreigners but whom medieval Londoners called 'aliens'. These were principally Flemings and Germans. The Italians had become especially unpopular and felt safer operating their important trade through Southampton.

The City was governed by a court of twenty-four aldermen representing the twenty-four wards, or ancient administrative divisions. Each year the aldermen elected one of their number to serve his turn as Mayor (the English title Lord Mayor first appears in 1414), and the aldermen came from their private houses to sit in what was already the Guildhall, or 'hall of the pleas of the City'. Like all medieval government, that of London had a strongly judicial flavour.

The class which produced the aldermen was composed of the very richest people, and these were the wholesalers and the dealers in precious and luxury goods. One of the world's great divides was between those who dealt wholesale, living in good houses where the ground-floor was sometimes a warehouse, and those who dealt retail, selling to the public from the narrow confines of a shop. (Those who bought retail in tiny quantities were of course often poorer still and Langland effectively contrasts these 'that piecemeal must buy' (C III 86) with the butchers, bakers and cookshop-keepers he accused of sharp practices.)

Men with skills were divided into gilds, of which there was a great number, constantly subdividing and amalgamating in struggles to advantage their members and restrict others. But the wholesalers' gilds were in reality companies of capitalists who operated the export-import trade, owned ships or shares in ships, ran their finances through credit by bills of exchange, managed the king's customs for him, and lived in close economic and even social connection with the royal court.

In the fourteenth century the dominant gilds were eight: mercers, grocers, drapers, fishmongers, goldsmiths, skinners, tailors and vintners. Originally these had plied the business denoted by their names, but there was no longer a necessary and exclusive link. For example, a man who once had made a fortune dealing in spices as a member of the pepperers' gild by the late fourteenth century would be a Grocer and might deal wholesale in anything. Those rich enough to get elected to the mastership of these gilds attired themselves in expensive 'liveries' and displayed their power and self-esteem by dining together, meeting in full panoply on important occasions, and taking care to exclude outsiders and the young or poor of their own craft. Gild, craft, mistery, company, these were all names denoting more or less the same thing, though 'company' soon became usual, and those who were 'of the livery' expected the deference due to those who could finance government itself. The Grocers made all their apprentices swear to be obedient 'to all the clothing of the fellowship in due reverence'.[19] All this was the sort of thing Langland hated, and it is not unfair to suppose that when he was

> . . . looth to reverencen
> Lords or ladies . . .   (B XV 5–6)

he was nominally following the Gospel advice to apostles: 'Salute no one in the road' (Luke 10:4) but likely as not both mocking the friars and enjoying his own eccentricity.

Langland's London was the meeting of worlds. Heaven met earth inside innumerable doors off the street before the Rood on the church screens. Court met city magnates in guarded chambers where the king could speak of great loans or some fine purchase. Rich met poor jostling out of doors; or across meal-tables as servants in the hall of noble or alderman placed the dishes; or, most starkly, in the court of criminal law where robed judges could see from their high bench, far below, the prisoners chained by the ankles.

But *Piers Plowman* presents not only the meeting of the different worlds but their distancing. The contrast is perhaps sharpest in London and pointed by the different treatment of royal Westminster and the town's taverns. This seems a result of no deliberate technique or careful poetic moral but rather a consequence of the writer's kind of perception. Confronted with institutions and officials he writes from outside and below; confronted with an individual he meets the eyes and comes alive.

The world of high society is revealed as a tableau in the Prologue. The king appears surrounded by nobles and counsellors, and in a few lines the poet describes the commonplace medieval view of society, composed of the various kinds of worker and ruled lawfully. A preacher speaks in Latin as from a high pulpit, pressing on the king the claims of mercy, and is followed by a talkative fellow who calls out that it is not a true king who does not try to maintain the laws, and he in turn is answered by a cry from the people that the king's orders were binding as law.

Perhaps these were real people as has been argued.[20] Perhaps Langland imagined or even saw the notabilities of the Good Parliament in 1376: Bishop Brunton and Speaker Peter de la Mare. Yet we can imagine the court scenes more readily from other surviving sources – Brunton's sermon text and the *Anonimalle Chronicle* – than from the shadowy figures of the poem and their abstract sentiments. Of the figures only two impress a keen image.

[19] Sylvia Thrupp, *op. cit.*, p. 29.
[20] G. R. Owst, 'The "Angel" and the "Goliardys" of Langland's Prologue', *Modern Language Review*, vol. 20 (1925), pp. 270–9.

One is the anonymous character kneeling in front of the king. We may speculate but not claim that it was Langland imagining himself to have been there –

> Thanne loked up a lunatik, a leene thyng withalle . . .
>
> (B Prol. 123)

In nine words we are told the moment of his action, his posture and his description.

The other is the lady Meed herself, another non-historical character, who glitters as one who has been visualized, fingers fretted with gold wire, and shortly made like a rider to mount a new-shod sheriff (B II 11,164).

This miniature contrast of images within the Westminster court may be extended to illustrate Langland's differing perceptions of the wider Westminster where great people ruled and the narrow London where they drank.

The late J. A. W. Bennett wrote that Langland's third Passus shows he knew Westminster intimately.[21] This may be true as far as the choreography goes. The figures are in place: king and courtiers, beadles and bailiffs. They receive Lady Meed in mock-courtly verse –

> Busked hem to the bour ther the burde dwellede
>
> [Repaired to her boudoir where the Lady lay]   (B III 14)

and then they proceed with the debate about her wedding which is a stylised comedy of manners. Yet the courtiers, their domestic friar, the king, and Conscience himself, indignant decliner of the suit, are little but lay figures. Only a reference to the Privy Seal, to poor people's miserable experience of the French wars, and the Lady's shower of florin bribes bring to the scene a tang of particular observation.

This lack of warm participation was not the fault of Westminster's character, which had power indeed to affect its true inhabitants, like Hoccleve, poet and official, who described his nervous reaction to the 'press' of people in Westminster Hall.[22] Langland did not live there, and he reels off the passers-by as they pop up like snap-shot targets, suitably alliterated: assizers, summoners, sheriffs and their clerks; bedels, bailiffs and brokers. The verbal inventiveness falls short of an eye-witness's detail.

In contrast with the world of Westminster, Glutton's drinking-bout on the way to church takes the reader or hearer into a living world (B V 297ff.). No matter that in the slightly earlier poem, *Winner and Waster*, there was also a

---

[21] J. A. W. Bennett, 'Chaucer's Contemporary', reprinted from S. S. Hussey, *Critical Approaches* (1969) in *The Humane Medievalist* (Rome, 1982), pp. 13–20.

[22] J. A. Burrow, 'Autobiographical poetry in the middle ages', *Proceedings of the British Academy*, vol. 68 (1982), pp. 404–5.

vivid tavern scene with a moral. If Langland had a model for his set-piece, his version has the sense of a life-drawing.

The paraphrase of this scene which ends the present chapter requires an excuse. It cannot be a substitute for Langland's lines, but even in modern English it invites comparison with another near-contemporary passage of street-observation. This is the description of the Great Revolt of 1381 in London, inserted into the *Anonimalle Chronicle* (see Note 18 above). It has been persuasively argued by its editor that the clerk who wrote this was an eye-witness, and was thinking in English though writing in Anglo-French. If so, the Revolt scene and the tavern scene share the characteristics of being written by clerks, in the vernacular, and conveying with little stylization the flow of gross conversation and crude action:

Next Glutton starts out to go to confession and heads for the church, but Bet the ale-wife hailed him and asked where he was off to.

'To church,' he said, 'I'm off to Mass and confession.'

'I've just opened a good barrel here, duck,' she said. 'Look, try that.'

'Got anything tasty?'

'Well, I've got some pepper and peony-seeds – a bit of garlic too,' she added, '– or a little bit of fennel-seed as it's a fast-day.'

Then Glutton went in, swearing God wouldn't mind. Cissy the shoemaker was sitting on the bench, also Wat the warren-keeper and his wife, Tim the tinker and two of his boys, Hick the horse-hire man and Hugh who sold pins and needles; and there were Clarice of Cock Lane and the parish clerk, also Father Peter himself and Peacock the Flemish bird, Davy the ditcher and a dozen others – a fiddler, a rat-catcher, one of the street-sweepers from Cheapside, a rope-maker, a messenger-lad and Rose from the hardware shop. Geoffrey of Garlickhithe was there too, and Taffy Griffin.

And a whole crowd of junk-dealers raised a cheer to give Glutton the old come-on.

Then Clement the cobbler took off his cloak for a game of New Fair and shouted out, 'any offers?', and Hick the horse man flung down his hood and asked Bet the butcher to bid for him.

Dealers were picked to fix a price and decide between hood and cloak, and they started whispering about this junk and arguing till Robin the rope-maker was asked to referee.

So Hick the ostler got the cloak and Clem had to be satisfied with a mugful and Hick's hood. Anyone who argued with the referee had to buy Glutton a gallon.

Everyone started laughing and scowling, and yelling, 'Fill them up', and so it went on till vespers and Glutton had had a skinful and kept farting and going out for a piss, and everyone held his nose and shouted 'what a stink!'

And old Glutton couldn't hardly walk or even stand up without a stick and started staggering sideways and backwards like a circus bitch or a bird-catcher fixing his lines; and when he got to the door his eyes glazed and he keeled over, and Clem the cobbler caught him just in time and heaved him up on his knees – Glutton was a big fellow – and then he went and threw up all over Clement and there wasn't a dog wouldn't have turned away from that muck. Heaving and struggling, his wife and the girl got him into bed where he lay like a corpse till Sunday evening . . . Then he sat up blearily and croaked, 'where's my beer-mug?' And at that his wife laid into him . . .

(from B V 297–364)

Chapter 3

THE RELIGIOUS SCENE

At the very beginning of *Piers Plowman* the writer presents himself as a solitary sort of man who is going out to look at the world. His vision took in many different sorts of people. No doubt much was interior vision – occurring, to put it plainly, within his own head as he brooded like Imaginatif, sitting by himself in sickness and health (B XII 2). But the historian who tries to see with Langland's eyes can hardly doubt that the poet in some way had sociable gifts and was able not only to entertain an audience but to communicate with the world in which he lived. Whether or not he had the soul of a hermit, he lived in society and wrote of the religious scene all about him.

In a general sense it was a Christian society which contained everybody, young and old, native and alien, the living and even the dead who were remembered and prayed for. In fourteenth-century England there were presumably few or no Jews, since they had been expelled by Edward I in 1290; people of other faiths must have been rare visitors, and 'heretics' when they appeared late in the century in Lollard form were certainly Christians.

The people belonged to the Christian church through the baptism of children, and nourished their common Christian life whenever they obeyed the great Lateran decree of 1215 requiring all but infants to receive Holy Communion at least once a year about Easter-time, having confessed to their own priest (*proprio sacerdoti*). The bishops who warned their flocks about the dangers of unwitnessed marriages were affirming that matrimony also was a Christian matter which must be public for the sake of stable unions and rightful heirs. Death was Christian too. At the end eveybody with the wretched exclusion of a few suicides and usurers ended up in hallowed earth. Notable people liked to arrange for their burial inside the church buildings, but as a rule bodies were mingled without fastidiousness:

At churche in the charnel cherles aren euele to know

(C VIII 45)

[In the church's burial place it's hard to tell master and man apart]

But if *Piers Plowman* was read by the devout, it was certainly not composed exclusively about them. Those whom the charitable pen of Langland described as his fellow-Christians (*emcristene*), meaning everyone, were spread over a very wide range of attitude. It was a religious age in the sense of breeding numbers of mystics and religious writers for the laity, religious too in the reference to God and His saints of the most worldly hopes and fears, and even in the habitual gestures of the conventional. It was irreligious, if the historian may guess, in the uninterest of the indifferent majority, and in this way much like any other age where religion does not form part of a political identity or find expression in brief mass excitements. Of his own country Langland wrote factually, 'most people who pass their lives on this earth have their treasure in this world and desire no better' (C I 6–7). It would seem that if men and women thought about their health, their property and those they loved, but rarely of religion, grasping only in occasional urgency at the promises of relic-mongers or the consolations of the spiritual world, they were much like the rest of mankind.

People encountered in *Piers Plowman* – peasants listening to the Pardoner in the pulpit, advocates arguing for their clients, and the tavern revellers themselves – were ordinary types preoccupied with getting and spending, and experience suggests they shade imperceptibly from virtual pagans to Christians by conviction. Langland wrote about them as his fellows who were expected by the church of their baptism to keep certain rules, whatever their station in life. Putting the rules in his own words, he gave them his own emphasis: live the life into which you are called; hear Mass (wholly) on Sundays and holy days; keep the fasting days if you are able. When you break the rules, repent and confess (C IX 219ff.).

Banal enough on recitation, the rules receive in Langland an immense bias towards repentance. It is a late medieval emphasis. At the dawn of Christianity, the patristic age was centred on the redeeming character of baptism, the unrepeatable cleansing and reception of the new believer. But the wear and tear of a world which was not ending in the Second Coming turned minds towards reconciliation for daily infidelities, and preoccupied them with contrition and making satisfaction.

Confession in general ceased to be a formidable public reconciliation after formidable public sins and became a private practice and thus in a way the dominant sacrament, gateway even to the Eucharist; and it is more continuously than any other the theme of *Piers Plowman*.

Confession became dominant – perhaps too dominant – because its practice became subtle, and most subtle when most genuine. Old tariffs of penances for crude lists of externally identifiable offences had before Langland's time been replaced by detailed manuals for confessors who had to gauge the culpability of the penitent, as indeed had the penitent too, to the best of his or her ability. Examination of conscience as a form of introspection carried the responsibility of judging the gravity of the offence and the degree of the sinner's understanding of and consent to it. And with normal human fallibility of judgment, it was no wonder there was room for argument about lax or scrupulous consciences and no wonder that penitents and confessors differed greatly amongst themselves.

If this small piece of church history seems tedious, it is none the less a key to understanding Langland who, without being an uncompassionate man, seems to have grown up with rather rigorous ideas about the practice of confession in his day.

Early in the poem confession receives an external description, as the queue of sinners lines up after repenting; but as time goes on, the seeker after Do Well is referred more deeply to the interior disposition of contrition. Often it is expressed in the scriptural imagery of tears, and this repeated insistence on water running from the eyes is hard for the literal-minded to accept, especially in the language of a Margery Kempe who advertised her devotion with tiresome sobs.

Langland, to do him justice, was concerned with the actuality, not demonstrations. As an honest man he cannot spell out a formulation of contrition, but he makes it clear that it is an interior disposition, and that it can up to a point be taught. 'How contrition [even] without confession comforts the soul, we see this in the psalter, for contrition catcheth away sin' (C XIV 115–6; ref. to Ps. 31). It is something the uninstructed man does not understand: 'the lewd man lies still and waits for Lent' (C XIV 120f.), he continues, and points out that even when he performs his Easter duties by going to confession he hasn't much contrition and hardly knows what to say, but stumblingly takes what his parish priest tells him, and that too is probably uninstructed.

Langland plays up the distinction between an instructed Christian and an ignorant one because he set great value on learning. Not that he held the crude idea that over-donnish theologians sometimes convey that God is specially available to the clever. On the contrary, he is at time almost despairing that the simple man can 'pierce heaven with a paternoster' while a life of study may leave the learned man on the shore. Langland is also very sarcastic about high-table theologians. His real point is that mere obedience to the regulation about annual confession cannot be a substitute for an attempts at repentance, and that people should be taught this. He speaks simply for interior Christianity.

*   *   *

If the religious scene in fourteenth-century England was numerically dominated by the indifferent, the conventional and the formal for whom Christianity was at most an annual routine, Langland himself was a striking
example of the devout individual who was also a conspicuous feature of the
age. They vary greatly. There were literate laymen of social standing with
private oratories, books of devotion, and spiritual directors;[1] perhaps
women of this category were even more numerous. There were the famous
mystics whose writings are still read: Richard Rolle; the sublime author of
the *Cloud of Unknowing*; and also before 1400 Walter Hilton and Dame
Julian of Norwich. Langland is uniquely outside these classes: not a priest,
not a layman, not a mystic, but a spiritual moralist and a poet. There were
also many solitaries in that age (of whom Langland may have been one,
anyhow for a time), and these were hermits (who might move around, like
Rolle) or anchorites who lived in authorized enclosure, perhaps in a
church-yard, or by a bridge. They were not the walled-up oddities of
horror-stories but 'holy' or 'separated' people encountered from the ancient
world onwards who might live eminently sane and not uncomfortable lives of
prayer and frugality and be available to anyone who wished to consult them.
There were also men of action like Sir John Clanvow who passed from
military life to that of a pilgrim: a transition seen in all ages.[2] All these in
their variety shared a likeness in belief in the repentance of which we have
been speaking or, to put it another way, in articulating the idea of conscience,
which is a strong feature of the age.

There was a more extreme segment of religious opinion. The personal
religion of repentance and the Biblical precepts of love were beginning at the
end of Langland's life to attract both gentle and simple people who would
shortly be called Lollards. By the time of John Wyclif's death in 1384 they
hardly formed part of the religious scene, but many people were ready to
listen to the preachers of a scriptural Christianity which rejected the physical
implications of a priestly religion: veneration of images and above all Christ
thought of as present in the Eucharistic elements of bread and wine. Some
thus inclined were of knightly status but many were men and women who
worked at artisan tasks, especially in the cloth-making regions of East
Anglia, the Chilterns, Kent, West Yorkshire, and also London and its
environs.

The important work of Anne Hudson has shown the love of English

---

[1] W. A. Pantin, 'Instruction for a devout and literate layman', in *Medieval Learning
and Literature*, ed. J. J. G. Alexander and M. T. Gibson (Oxford, 1976), pp. 398
–422; Anthony Goodman, 'The piety of John Brunham's daughter, of Lynn', in
Medieval Women, ed. Derek Baker (Studies in Church History: Subsidia 1.
Ecclesiastical History Society 1978), pp. 347–58.

[2] V. J. Scattergood, 'The Two Ways: an unpublished religious treatise by Sir John
Clanvowe', in *English Philological Studies* X (1967), pp. 33–56.

literacy which suffused Lollardy from the start, and it is hard not to think of Langland as part of the same world in which literacy and the apprehension of quite sophisticated religious ideas was the portion of inheritance among many with few worldly goods. In a very diluted sense Langland was a spiritual kinsman: in hostility to the worldly power of the clergy, to arrogant Church lordship, to the clink of money round the altar.

But in Langland the core of orthodoxy remained intact. His objection to the endowed church was the conceit of its beneficiaries, not the system of benefices. He hated the taint of bribery, not the crozier of a good bishop. He spoke of pilgrimages, rosaries and prayers for the dead with respect, and if he snarled at misemployed popes he safeguarded the authority of their office: 'this is part of our belief, as lettered men teach us' (B VII 176). Anti-clericalism is not equivalent to unorthodoxy.

To Lollards much of the apparatus of Catholic religion was unscriptural; their understanding rested upon the Gospels and Epistles, shorn of interpretations which involved church ceremonies and institutions but informed with a concern for practical goodness and love of Christ.

Some have seen the Lollard emotional commitment as inward-turning, to the family groups from which domineering priestly ceremonies could be excluded and the strength of womanly personalities allowed to unfold; and probably many inner needs were expressed in this way, as family members known to each other celebrated Christian mysteries within a domestic but not canonical enclosure, without priests but with a priesthood that in a quite unformulated way was felt to belong to all members.

Something of this emerges in the words of Elizabeth Stamford, a pupil of the Chiltern Lollard, Thomas Bele:

> . . . that Christ feedeth and fast nourisheth his church with his own precious body, that is, the bread of life coming down from heaven: this is the worthy word that is worthily received, and joined unto men to be in one body with him. Sooth it is that they both be one: they may not be parted: this is the wisely deeming of the holy sacrament, Christ's own body: this is not received by chewing of teeth but by hearing with ears and understanding with your soul, and wisely working thereafter . . .[3]

In fact it is through phrases like this, warmly emotional and nearly sacramental in imagery, that we see the distance between Lollards and Langland. Langland dwells little upon his own dispositions before the Eucharist but insists, unlike the Lollards, in a brisk and practical way upon regular confession and communion. Admittedly his Christianity is an interior religion and capable of moments of joy. But his poem is constantly

---

[3] Claire Cross, 'Great Reasoners in Scripture: the activities of women Lollards, 1380–1530', in *Medieval Women* (as in Note 1), pp. 359–80. For the major work on Lollards, Anne Hudson, *Lollards and their Books* (1985), and *The Premature Reformation* (1989).

embellished, indeed supported, by a clerk's liturgical Latin, and so far from sharing the warmth of divine love in words with his Kate, he pushes her to kneel with him in front of the Rood. The comparison separates Lollard folk with their priesthood of all believers from Langland, scourge of ignorant curates but himself a clerk.

One of the interesting questions about the religious scene is in just this matter – the extent to which clerks and laity felt themselves to be of separate orders. It is a vast subject, but in this context it should at least be said that the 'coming of the literate layman' in no way overturned ancient clerical society. The priest with his Flemish wench in the tavern would be pointless without the hope of a shocked laugh. A century later a citizen financed a 'perpetual commonalty' of the seven chantry priests of St James Garlickhithe (round the corner from Glutton's brew-shop), saying that these chaplains 'conversed among laymen and wandered about rather than dwelt among clerks, as was decent'.[4] Langland shared in that clerical world, not by priesthood but in the measure of his learning, the 'portion of his inheritance', and worshipped in church through the liturgical year.

*   *   *

For the ordinary Christian the centre was the parish or, more exactly, the parish church. Already at the time of the Domesday Survey in 1086 the endowment of parish churches in country settlements allowed most people to attend week by week. Through the twelfth and thirteenth centuries the increasing population, and its wealth and building skills, provided new chapels which might receive parochial status, while existing churches were often enlarged. Villagers needed less often to make difficult journeys to get married or bury their dead, and a multiplication of altars permitted the celebration of Mass more frequently at their wish. In London especially, wealth and the concentration of many different communities meant an extraordinary number of parish churches. By Langland's day there were over one hundred.

Originally, landlords had founded churches on their estates to support their mass-priests, but the property given was thought of as belonging, under God, to the saint of the church's dedication, a relic of whom had been placed under the altar-stone by the consecrating bishop.

So the land given to endow a parish church, known as the glebe, had an immortal proprietor and could not be disposed of at the will of priest, patron or other living person. It was the parson's during his life and helped to support him.

Whether a glebe was large or small was an accident of history. A parish church's main income came from the tithes of the parishioners, obligatory

---

[4] A. Hamilton Thompson, *The Historical Growth of the English Parish Church* (Cambridge, 1913), p. 26.

since the tenth century. In theory this was the payment from each household of a tenth part of what had been gained during the year by 'natural increase', and although we hear sometimes of strange tithes like pairs of manufactured gloves, by far the most important sort was the tithe of corn: the greater tithe. The priest who enjoyed this income as the saint's representative was known as the rector. He might normally drive his cart into the fields of his parish at harvest time, load up every tenth sheaf and haul them off to his tithe barn.

But in England it became common for lords actually to 'appropriate' (= give or sell) parish churches to monasteries and sometimes to colleges. When this happened the recipient became the rector, but had to ensure proper service of the parish by putting in a deputy, or 'vicar'. The vicar was supposed by canon law to be paid suitably, and usually got something like a third of the income. Some of this would be offerings made, as now, for conducting marriages and burials, or on a regular basis as a Christian duty.

Important London parishes mostly remained rectories and were additionally rich through the contributions of wealthy parishioners. They often became the livings of especially favoured priests, either learned men or able administrators in the service of the great. Though destroyed by the Fire and rebuilt by Wren the names of some are still famous: St Mary le Bow (or 'of the Arches'), All Hallows Bread Street, off Cheapside, or, for instance, St Michael Paternoster Royal, whose 'Royal' was a rendering of *in Riola*, 'belonging to La Réole' in Bordeaux whose wine-merchants once worshipped there as expatriates.

In parishes like these the routine priestly work was also often done by a substitute, and when Langland went to Mass in London he would probably hear the priest known as the 'parish chaplain'. But it was generally possible to hear notable preachers at one church or the other, or at 'Paul's Cross' just outside the cathedral, and such sermons sometimes had strong political messages. People were easily excited and could express themselves, for example, by witholding alms or changing priests.

There were also chantry chaplains, usually connected with town churches, and very numerous in London, and they earned their living from bequests and endowments, administered by trustees, in return for saying the specified Masses and prayers.

The fourteenth-century parish world was just as socially divided as that of Trollope's Barsetshire, and probably more volatile. In any cathedral city you could find the equivalents of cathedral dignitaries and canons (with fur on their robes), rich rectors, often away on business, modest vicars, and large numbers of unbeneficed clergy who, without the protected tenure of a living, worked in various ways for fees and stipends. This is to say nothing of the great number of medieval clergy who were really the equivalent of civil servants, from clerks in the royal household down to the chaplain who did the accounts or wrote letters for some affluent household.

Yet Barsetshire is a long way from Langland's parish world. We have to think away much of the nineteenth century in trying to approach the fourteenth, and at moments when we think we have done this we discover we still do not know. There is, for example, the problem of clerical ignorance. Poor clergy in nineteenth-century England must have been in most ways incomparably more educated than their earlier counterparts; yet, when Langland writes harshly about 'ignorant vicars' his standards both of doctrine and spirituality seem very high. Nor can we recapture the climate of preaching and prayer created by unmarried men, schooled in no seminary or theological college. We have anecdotes and vignettes: Father Peter in the tavern or the gentle Clerk of Oxenford with his little hoard of books. Beyond such things we can speak only of certain conditions and rules, historically verifiable, under which they lived.

By Langland's time the atmosphere of parish life was much altered by movements little more than a hundred years old. One was competition from friars who attracted relatively large numbers of able young men into priestly ministry. It is arguable how many of these would otherwise have become ordinary parochial clergy, but their quality inevitably had strong effects in parishes. They will require closer attention later in this book for their crucial effect on Langland, but at this point perhaps the perseverance of the parish clergy themselves is to be admired, for all the abuse they have attracted, as they with their congregations were struggling towards greater literacy.

The second movement of change is allied to this, namely, the increasing role of leading lay parishioners as managers of parish matters. As churchwardens they had custody of funds, sometimes even in competition with the priest. They frequently supervised the good order of the church structure other than the chancel. They were active as trustees for monies left to pious uses in the increasing numbers of wills left by parishioners.

Let us return to the physical condition of the parish. In some ways the fourteenth century was a golden age by reason of the wealth accruing to people of middling status through the economic activity noted in the previous chapter. To the availability of this wealth were joined two other conditions. One was the deep belief in Purgatory as a somehow transient stage of suffering in satisfaction for sins forgiven but not paid for; prayer for these 'holy souls' as they were called was organized on a great scale through the setting up of chantry foundations. The other condition was the development of the legal trust by which properties could be sold and the proceeds conveyed to pious objects. Not only that, but wills at this time witness to a stream of bequests to parochial objects 'for tithes forgotten'. In both these ways the idea of rendering back what you owe was a dominant theme. It was not Langland's private motto, though to him a burning text.

Out of these funds the parish church and its environs were improved. There were sometimes new images, innumerable tapers and lights, and almsdeeds of a social character which follow quite a common form in the wills and testaments drawn for local people. Langland knew the phrases well, whether or not he ever acted as a scribe, and he put them into the mouth of Truth, who commanded merchants, 'mend those roads in dreadful disrepair, and decayed bridges too; provide food for the poor and for prisoners; contribute to funds for young girls' dowries when they get married or become nuns; and set scholars to school' (B VII 27–31).

Romantic nineteenth-century pictures of the Angelus being said in the fields sometimes convey the impression that the medieval steeple or tower with its bells signified to the parish landscape the spot where Christ in the Eucharistic bread was contained in the pyx by the altar. True, the devotion of Corpus Christi was beginning its long history. But if one could step inside the door of Langland's parish church, it would at a guess be neither the altar nor the sanctuary light that commanded attention but the Rood, mounted aloft on its screen between nave and chancel. This was the great crucifix, its figure now generally in an attitude of suffering, flanked by those of the Virgin and of St John the beloved disciple. Not much except the Rood's large scale can be told from the few surviving screens, like that of Welsh Newton near Hereford (c.1320). But the medieval Rood stretched across the width of the church, and a narrow stair and gangway allowed lights to be placed on the parapet below the Calvary. Whatever other statues there were, the Rood was especially illuminated by wax candles. More than the Sacrament it seems to have been the central focus of devotion. Some Roods were objects of local pilgrimage: for instance, of the twenty authorized pilgrimages in East Anglia, Roods and crosses were the most common, more so than images of the Virgin.[5] It is in keeping that the 'Revelations of Divine Love' of the contemporary mystic, Dame Julian of Norwich, should have centred visually on the physical suffering of the Crucified. Fourteenth-century devotion was not only Christocentric but attracted to the lineaments of a man, stained with a man's blood. Langland's Envy, in his malicious manner, described how he misused his devotions:

> And whan I come to the kirk and sholde knele to the Roode
> And preye for the peple as the preest techeth . . .
> Thanne I crye on my knees that Crist yyve hem sorwe . . .
> (B V 103–6)

And at the poem's crisis there appears Christ bleeding in the framework of the church before the people: 'in the midst of Mass I fell asleep and suddenly dreamed that Piers the Plowman was painted all bloody, and came in with a cross before the common people' (B XIX 5–7).

In a modern setting a parish church like Welsh Newton appears extremely small, and offers a welcoming intimacy to the city visitor. But to the

[5] Norman P. Tanner, *The Church in late medieval Norwich* (Toronto, 1984), p. 85.

medieval villager his parish church was spacious and firm by contrast with the cottages round about. It might be in disrepair, but its uninterrupted use proved it a good, weathertight space for the community's needs, its floor covered with rushes or straw and the moveable furnishings pushed back to leave room for all manner of events and functions that could be accommodated nowhere else.

Bishops on their visitations did not always approve. In fourteenth-century Barking (East London) games, dances, wrestlings and other sports were held in both the parish and the convent churches.[6] It was common for feasts to be celebrated in churches with trestle-tables set up in the nave. In some larger churches periodic markets might be held and stalls erected by merchants down the middle. The parish chaplain on such occasions might authorize a subordinate to sleep in the church at night on guard, though the vicar of Colyton in Devon was probably unusual in part-using his church as brew-phouse and corn-store.

By the time Langland and Chaucer were writing some churches at least were furnished with pulpits, from which visiting preachers like pardoners as well as the incumbent could speak to the people. Some also had pews. Wrath in a female embodiment speaks of how in church

> Amonges wyves and wydewes y am woned to sitte
> Yparroked in pues . . .   (c vi 143–6)

> [Amongst wives and widows I am accustomed to sit, paddocked into pews]

and how she was seized with irritation when her neighbour received the holy bread before her.

The intrusion of the medieval world into the parish church was only a secondary matter to its role as the centre of worship through prayer and the sacraments. The most important act was the celebration of the Mass by the parish chaplain, which he was supposed to perform every day. The laity were required to be present on Sundays and certain other holy days throughout the year, when pious people might also attend matins and evensong. No statistics were recorded to tell us how well attendances were kept. *Piers Plowman* refers to absenteeism and the rush for the door as the celebrant neared the end. It also suggests that the laity may have received Communion at the end of Mass:

> I went to church to hear wholly the mass and to receive communion afterwards   (B XIX 3–5)

---

[6] For some of this material see J. R. H. Moorman, *Church Life in England in the Thirteenth Century* (Cambridge, 1946). This book was constructively reviewed by C. R. Cheney in *Journal of Theological Studies*, vol. 47 (1946), pp. 99–104.

though this may be no more than a reference to the normal distribution of Communion towards the end of the liturgy. In any case Langland's text seems to confirm that it was a special occasion and that even a devout layman would not expect to receive Communion every time he went to Mass.

If the Mass was the principal act of worship, penance was, as we have seen, the sacrament which dominated the lives and thoughts of Christians at this time. It is frequently portrayed in illuminated manuscripts, sometimes in ways which mingle mockery with awe. Before the days of confessional boxes, the penitent is shown kneeling, mouth to the ear of the priest who sits with head bent and averted. Perhaps the painter might show a friar-confessor with a demon grimacing on his other side.

Pictures which mock confession or suggest easy penances would have had no meaning, however, if the population had ignored the practice of religion. The historians who argue that medieval religion for most people was merely a matter of folk-lore, untouched by any sense of individual conscience until the rigorist indoctrinations of the Reformation and Counter-Reformation, have arrived at the wrong conclusion by collecting examples of local superstitions.

Then there were the hand-books for confessors which were being copied and used by priests, like that by Thomas of Chobham,[7] a huge and systematic compilation of all the offences imaginable – and some not – with their subdivided degrees of culpability and the appropriate penances. The books like this are also evidence of the universal medieval sense of guilt, just as is the Pardoner, to be encountered shortly, with the hopes he seemed to offer of getting off the punishment deserved by sin.

In a way the medieval church organized a sort of tug-of-war for the souls of its people: the strict and learned study of canon law to be applied in parish confessionals for the menacing correction of sinners versus the encouraging words of equally skilful men who could deal gently with anyone who showed the slightest sign of mending his ways. On the side-lines stood both easy-going and stern characters – genial friars and gravely warning Langland – persuading people in somewhat differing tones how they ought to react.

Whichever side was taken, the battle to persuade the public was fought by preaching. Sermons occupied a place in life hardly imaginable today. Popes and bishops who were always reproving the parish clergy for their ignorance

---

[7] F. Broomfield (ed.), *Thome de Chobham Summa Confessorum* (Analecta Medievalia Namurcensis, vol. 25 (1968). Educated clergy had been actively writing about the guiding of consciences of penitents since c.1200. The friars especially were concerned as much about individual spiritual problems as about legalistic rules, and Langland's criticism of them seems coloured by his overall anger at the apparently unjust distribution of wealth in his own changing times. See T. N. Tentler, 'The Summa for Confessors as an instrument of social control' in *The Pursuit of Holiness in late medieval and renaissance religion*, ed. Charles Trinkaus with Heiko A. Obermann (Leiden, 1974), pp. 103–37.

were in reality insisting on an improved standard of popular instruction. Doubtless many country clergy were ineffective either because they were torpid or because they were little removed from simple peasants. But the universities and the friars had from soon after 1200 been setting enormously higher standards.

Sermons were preached at distinctly different levels, adapted to occasion and hearers. The university sermon was at the intellectual pinnacle, a regular exercise for professional scholars, argued in set logical form and supported at every stage by authoritative texts from Scripture and the Fathers. Political sermons were another type, preached often at moments of crisis before the king or at an open-air sermon arena like St Paul's Cross hard by the cathedral. Here the talking was in the vernacular, aimed at inflaming or calming the people or justifying some political act. For the majority of people without education the sermons of the friars were lively instructions, illustrated with anecdotes and parables, and in London they attracted many people into the new friar churches with their large naves and prominent pulpits.

Sermons played a large part in the formation of mentalities not only from lack of the sort of competition we have today, but also because they were treated as of prime importance by authorities everywhere. A learned man like Gabriel Biel in Germany could argue that the sermon came even before the Mass because faith comes from hearing.

The parish sermon has been belittled by historians who have accepted the criticisms made by medieval councils and bishops as the whole truth. They set a pretty high standard. A famous directive sent out by John Pecham the archbishop of Canterbury in 1281 was called 'The Ignorance of Priests' from its opening words. To the archbishop himself the material probably seemed elementary, but then he was a Parisian professor (and also a friar). Knowing the training value of dividing everything into numbered headings to be learned, he laid down that priests were to get by heart and teach their congregations: the Fourteen Articles of faith (i.e. the Apostles' Creed), the Ten Commandments, the Seven Principal Virtues, the Seven Deadly Sins, the Seven Sacraments, the Seven Works of Mercy and the Two Gospel Precepts which are, of course, the love of God and love of neighbour which are basic to *Piers Plowman*. The instruction was extended to the province of York by Archbishop Thoresby in 1357, and a monk of St Mary's, York, made an expanded English version in rhyme.[8]

William Langland's case against ignorant curates who led their people astray were not grounded, to do him justice, on a celestially impossible level of knowledge, but rather on the observation that Christian folk were not encouraged systematically in their faith or taught to be generous with their

---

[8] W. A. Pantin, *The English Church in the Fourteenth Century* (Cambridge, 1955), pp. 211–12.

property or sorry for their sins (B X 74–5). In fact he ascribed this to moral not intellectual ignorance, and considered it part of the fashion for mere cleverness followed by a lot of priests, especially friars, to indulge in philosophical arguments with cold hearts and condescend to the simple with undemanding tales.

Parish life was lived through sacraments, sermons and socializing, but it should hardly go without saying that it was about faith in Christ, who enters the world in narrative form. The parish was therefore also a vehicle for the re-enactment of a narrative year by year. The one God who spoke to the Jewish people through lawgivers and prophets appeared in time – so the Christian world agreed – as a child who grew up to proclaim himself the promised redeemer, taught, and was arrested and executed by crucifixion.

The events of the suffering and death of Christ chronicled in the Gospels and known as the Passion provided the central theme of parish worship. The readings at Mass and the offices of Matins and Vespers varied Sunday by Sunday, even day by day, to commemorate the stages of the story and its setting within the past history of Jewish prophecy. If simple people could not follow the outline, as is sometimes alleged, the critical moments of the Holy Week before Easter were presented to them in theatrical form by the ceremonies laid down in the liturgy.

Palm Sunday saw leaves or foliage distributed to the congregation, in commemoration of Christ's entry into Jerusalem on a mule or donkey, when the crowd cheered and threw welcoming palm leaves on the road before him. In some churches the feet of twelve poor men were symbolically washed by the priest on the Thursday in mime of Christ's act as he demonstrated on his disciples his universal commandment to love one another. On Good Friday a crucifix was placed on the chancel steps before the congregation who approached on their knees – 'creeping to the cross' – to kiss the figure. And at Easter the bells were rung again to mark the end of Lent and the celebration of the Lord's resurrection from the tomb.

Piers Plowman is constructed round the story. The poem is not just a mirror of the Christian year or a dramatization of the liturgy, as has sometimes been argued. But it presents the Passion as a climax to months of preparation which the poet as parishioner experienced Sunday by Sunday in his local church. The drawn-out end of the poem, too, has a spiritual likeness to the long summer months from Easter round again to Advent when the struggle of Christian life goes on and souls are tended for the barn of Holy Church just as the sheaves from the fields were in actually harvested into the village barns of England.

*   *   *

It is among the commonest human experiences to see members of your own side as enemies. Successful refusal ever to do this would no doubt do away with paranoia, but would also abolish self-criticism. But every now and then a great writer appears whose hates, justified or not, are part of his own message. Langland was one of these.

No one who reads *Piers Plowman* can escape the constant naming of enemies among those who might also be thought by the historian to be working for the Christian redemption. They gather at the end of the poem in the 'great host against Conscience' (B XX 113). Three of them may be singled out, not because they are sinful or bad practitioners of their trades, like cheating hucksters or ignorant vicars, but because their very professions are thought of as perverse, though masquerading as the service of Christ's church. They are the friars, the pardoners and the church lawyers who operated the ecclesiastical courts and especially their matrimonial jurisdiction. In each case the basic charge is that they took money in return for spurious spiritual goods and services.

Langland was obsessed with the friars. Living in an age accustomed to different kinds of anti-clericalism, his violence was greater than that of most. Papal taxation, jealousies about benefices, tithes, political bishops, monastic landlords – all these hurt the purse and could be envisaged as somehow improvable. But to Langland the friars were intimately the deceivers of men and women, recipients of alms freely given to sustain work thought heavenly.

In the middle of the poem there is an elaborate scene which epitomises the writer's view. He is wandering over the earth for a long time begging his bread, 'in the manner of a mendicant' (B XIII 1ff.) he adds in a significant qualification; and he is ruminating on the way fortune had failed him. In the sequence of his thought he lights first upon the threat of old age, and then immediately upon the friars – how they followed folk who were rich and set the poor at little price and refused them burial in their churches unless they had left them money, and how – the voice seems to rise – their covetousness overcomes clerks and priests, and thus simple people are led by ignorant priests to incurable pains.

As the poet falls into his fourth Vision, he is invited by Conscience to a dinner-party where the other guests are Learning, Patience and a great divine in the place of honour, who (in C XV 30) turns out to be a friar. In the set-piece debate which follows, the master-friar guzzles and swills and, pushing away his empty dishes, holds forth on the importance of learned teaching, brushing aside what Patience tries to say about love. Donnishly he dismisses the stupid guest from his notice and settles down, flushed, to an evening's intelligent conversation with Learning.

It is interesting that conversation at a well-loaded dinner-table is a favourite scene with Langland, almost a stock property for the playing of his major obsession with those who speak of divinity in a frivolous or hypocritical way instead of listening to sincere speakers (presumably like himself) (cf. C VII 105–7; C XI 31–41). It was also a set where friars could be mocked for their fabled likeness to the Pharisees enjoying their places of honour and deferential treatment (e.g. Mt. 23:6–7).

In any case, this painful scene brings together strands of feeling about the friars: their learning, their social acceptability, self-confidence, arrogance and supposed greed in the presence of food and drink. It is a plausible and displeasing picture which by the time Langland wrote had been a long time swimming into focus.

The Franciscan and Dominican friars came to England in the 1220s, almost as soon as they were founded, and they established themselves, as did the other orders of friars, Carmelites and Augustinians, a little later, in centres of population and influence. They attracted bright young men and quickly became popular with aristocratic and other well-to-do people. With good minds, trained for learning and preaching, they drew congregations and support.

But though they excelled over parish-priests in the general skill of their mission, it would be wrong to think of the friars as the only clergy of ability in the thirteenth and fourteenth centuries. It was an age of intellectual achievement. The universities at Oxford and Cambridge were enjoying their first golden age and their lecture-halls were hearing masters who were rightly admired for their brilliance, not only in formal theology but in philosophy, logic and mathematics. Some were friars, like the Franciscan William of Ockham, others secular clergy like John Wyclif, a galaxy of talent whose disputes, often bitter, could help to sharpen wits as well as blunt sensibilities. As always, there were scores of others able to gain high preferment in the church or lucrative office in the realm, but who may be reckoned just below the highest standards of intellect. Many, from the best downwards, were below the optimum standard of humility.

Such a society breeds self-admiration and mutual jealousy. It breeds also, almost as a mode of relaxation, a kind of professional game-playing with ideas which can keep a high table amused but, carried negligently outside, can depress and scandalize a simpler public. It would be priggish to deny logicians their witty recreations, but trouble comes if the same men who in general account themselves keepers of consciences, prove themselves to be supercilious and allow themselves to be overheard. The damage is compounded if they take themselves so seriously that they lecture when they are billed to preach:

> Freres and fele othere maistres that to the lewed men prechen,
> Ye moeven materes unmesurable to tellen of the Trinite,
> That oftetymes the lewed peple of hir bileve doute . . .
>
> (B XV 70–2)

> [Friars and many other masters who preach to unlearned men! You stir up matters beyond the reach of reason to talk abstrusely about the Trinity. Little wonder that unlearned people often come to doubt their faith.]

Much better, continued the poet, to abandon this tone of voice and stick to the Ten Commandments and the Seven Sins.

Jealousies were chiefly polarized between the friars and the secular clergy. Their differences of intellectual style just alluded to form no doubt a fairly superficial layer in this history of a major conflict, though it is useful in the present context to highlight the personal feelings experienced by Langland and, indeed, by other religious writers aware of the dazzling effects of contemporary subtle scholarship.[9]

There is a material base to most chronic hostilities, and the conflict with the friars was no exception. The friars' own rules forbade them to acquire land, and they lived mainly by begging, at which they were often very skilled.

From the start they had to beg for somewhere to live as well as for their daily bread. From houses given them in poor suburbs they often moved up to convents in town-centres with fine churches attached. By popular preaching, hearing confessions attentively and knowing how to talk to different kinds of people they gained the affections and support of the laity, poor as well as rich, to such an extent that parish priests felt threatened in livelihood and *amour propre*.

Every house of friars appointed collectors, known also as 'limitors', to walk round a defined area asking for contributions in food and, by the fourteenth century, money; in return they might promise the saying of Mass or prayers and even the 'confraternity' of their convent which pious people might value for the sense of spiritual friendship it could give. Abuses existed, like a system spotted by Chaucer by which a friar with over-developed business instincts could agree to pay his convent a regular sum and then keep the proceeds of begging for his own disposal. Another was to have the friar and his companion carry sacks stuffed with offerings in unseemly profusion.

These may have been exceptions. The records tell of many poor friars who also served the poor. But it is usually the flamboyant cases that make news and, in the fourteenth century, kindled satire and anticlericalism. Langland himself made play with the beggar who asked for meals and also filled up his sack.

Unfortunately, the friars did more than beg their living according to Gospel example, and more than beg with professional organization. They turned it all into a theory. From the New Testament texts recommending a life of great simplicity many friars chose to understand begging as the most perfect form of the religious life and a mirror of Christ's own life-style.

It was bad enough to have élite religious orders scooping up offerings and

---

[9] 'The Epistle of Privy Counsel' in Clifton Wolters (ed.), *The Cloud of Unknowing and other works* (Penguin Classics, 1978 and reprinted), p. 163.

penetrating to the living-quarters of citizens. It was intolerable when their subjects held forth that Christ and his disciples had been absolute beggars who lived entirely from alms, and that therefore the mendicants were superior in profession to other clergy, the more so as this self-assurance by no means lessened the esteem in which important layfolk held them.

Together with these different kinds of success, the admiration that sprang from it, and the apparent self-admiration which followed the friars' own estimation of their vocation, there came also a form of wealth. Of course living-standards, if they rise, take the world with them, and it would be utopian to expect the austerities of charismatic founders to be followed exactly by future generations of followers. But leaving aside the special history of the Spiritual Franciscans, it seems likely that the numerous fourteenth-century followers of Francis and Dominic were housed and clothed well beyond a decent minimum.[10] Gifts had been pressed upon them for decades.

The London Franciscans as a central example may stand for others. Their earliest lodging in 1224 had been a rented house in Cornhill, a thoroughfare Langland himself later described as his home. But the London citizens quite soon provided their friars with a better site, north of Newgate Street, and rich merchants like the Mercers built them fine quarters with running water. The royal family itself gave a new, large church, and when Langland was living in London the Franciscan convent was housing between sixty and ninety friars, some of them highly qualified university masters, and many of them engaged in lucrative begging. Their house had just completed a series of thirty-six stained-glass windows, and their hall was a place where the nobility was said to meet. The reproofs of Langland and sarcasm of Chaucer have to be read against a genuine popularity of the friars, especially among the affluent, but also among moderately prosperous people whose wills record bequests to the friars year after year. It is hardly sufficient explanation to say that bequests to the friars were merely a pious custom. The custom itself was a response to an institution sober folk thought worth having.

This brief sketch should help to explain why so many clergy, especially among the seculars who moved between universities and parishes, could not love the friars. The seculars themselves numbered in their ranks men of intellect and polemical skill. In an age which created theories to justify situations, it was quite in keeping that mendicant arguments about Christ's poverty should be matched by secular arguments about mendicant wickedness. In fact a powerful myth was created that the friars were part of a plot. It fitted in well with the older myth that the end of the world would be heralded by the appearance of 'Antichrist'.

[10] A. G. Little, 'The Failure of Mendicancy', in *Studies in English Franciscan History* (Manchester, 1917).

Systematic attacks on the friars by the secular clergy began at the University of Paris in the 1250s, and were never surpassed in violence or theoretical completeness. The champion of the secular masters was a theologian called William of St Amour, who preached against the friars and in 1255 issued a notorious book called *The Perils of the Last Times*.

These works made skilful use of New Testament texts and later commentaries to make people believe that the friars were in fact those plausible deceivers said to be expected just before the coming of 'Antichrist' and the end of the world. The way these ideas affected *Piers Plowman* will in due course be looked at in the last chapter. Their arrival on the English religious scene needs brief explanation here.[11]

The Gospels contain severe indictments of the Pharisees and also discourses by Christ on the coming destruction of Jerusalem and the end of the world. This material is especially prominent in Matthew, chapters 23 and 24. In the long medieval tradition about the end of the world and the Second Coming of Christ it was held that people would be deceived by apparently devout persons, variously called 'hypocrites' or 'antichrists', who would turn out to be the enemies of Christ himself. One of William of St Amour's strokes of genius was to use the Pharisees, so terribly threatened for their self-righteousness, hypocrisy and greed, as the very types of the friars. There were key-ideas in the Gospel which clicked in the minds of medieval men as they watched the mendicants at work and play. As in Matthew 23:1–7, the Pharisees were great layers-down of the Law; they didn't practise from the heart what they preached; they liked attention, especially having the top place at banquets and being called 'Rabbi' or Master, both when preaching and when promenading in the market-place.

All this was made to fit the friars. But it is important to distinguish two elements, both in William of St Amour and in those who followed him: one is the theorizing about the imminent end of the world, the other is the attack on friars. It is the second of these which seems historically much the more important in the literature, in the preaching, and presumably the thoughts of the time. The animosity against the mendicants, however unchristian we may think it, had good reasons behind it, as has been explained. Evidence of real apocalyptic excitement, in the mass or even in individuals, is more elusive.

So anti-friar feeling ran high in the late thirteenth century and through the fourteenth. It entered the writing of the French poets Jean de Meung and Rutebeuf; it was shouted in the schools and discussed perhaps more quietly in monasteries; like other ideas it crossed the Channel without the slightest difficulty, passing into influential reference manuscripts and from masters to the ears of pupils. As men of zeal and eloquence the friars replied. In the

---

[11] For a comprehensive discussion of medieval hostility towards the friars, Penn R. Szittya, *The Antifraternal Tradition in Medieval Literature* (Princeton, 1986).

1320s the pope (John XXII) condemned their theory and practice of poverty which gave more ammunition to their enemies. It was vigorously asserted that the Easter confessions ought to be made to one's *parish* priest; also that able-bodied men who went round begging were harming those who were handicapped and really had to beg: a telling point on the morrow of a great famine. The idea was heard more stridently that friars gave easy penances, an accusation easy to make and probably hard to prove, but certainly bishops became annoyed at friars who heard confessions without the formality of getting permission, and in 1358 the bishop of Exeter joined up the two bits of polemic to call the friars in his diocese *hypocriti* and heralds of Antichrist.

In England the most violent campaign against the friars was launched by Richard FitzRalph, a native of northern Ireland who became archbishop of Armagh,[12] and was one of several Oxford-educated Anglo-Irishmen to become hard anti-mendicants. He was, incidentally, a pupil and friend of Bishop Grandison of Exeter.

FitzRalph was one of those many influential characters in history who experience conversion with a vengeance. He had been acquainted since boyhood with the friars and was aware of their work in preaching and hearing confessions among the Gaelic-speaking poor in Ulster, both before and during the Black Death of 1348–9. His hostility developed suddenly, and in 1350 he was preaching against the friars in front of the pope at Avignon on the text 'Remain in the state to which you are called' (I Cor. 7:20), the selfsame text used by Langland later in his 'autobiographical' *Passus*, where he justified his own continuance in his rather odd clerical way of life. FitzRalph used the accusation that the friars presumed to be especially Christ-like in their begging, and that they curried favour by giving absolution on easy terms, sometimes without requiring their penitents to make restitution.

In England FitzRalph preached a series of tough vernacular sermons in various churches, including that of Burford near Oxford (in 1347), Barking in east London and, by invitation of its Dean, at St Paul's London in 1357. In these discourses a leading accusation was that friars failed to love their neighbours, by which he meant the ordinary parish clergy who had 'cure of souls' – the 'curates' – and with this went the complaint that rich London parishioners were failing to pay their tithes but heaping alms upon the friars.

FitzRalph was the amplifier of anti-friar tradition. Those who did not hear his sermons could read what he said in his Latin *Defence of the Curates* which was widely circulated. Eighty-four manuscripts of it have so far been

---

[12] Katherine Walsh, *A fourteenth-century scholar and primate: Richard FitzRalph in Oxford, Avignon and Armagh* (Oxford, 1981). See also J. R. H. Moorman, *A History of the Franciscan Order* (Oxford, 1968), esp. ch. 27. Wendy Scase in her *'Piers Plowman' and the new Anticlericalism* (Cambridge, 1989) in my view overstates her case.

discovered,[13] and it was translated into English by John Trevisa, possibly when he was a Fellow of Queen's College, Oxford, between 1369 and 1378.

'Remain in your vocation' – 'love your neighbour' – 'render back what you owe': it is interesting to note these great Langland themes being preached across the land just as he was writing his poem.

The early charges against the friars levelled by William of St Amour have the stamp of jealousy polished to fanaticism, and it is not hard to see how such eloquent and sustainable passions could have been conveyed down the generations of university masters and spread to a wider circle by both oral and written tradition.

Their evident impact on Langland will be discussed in the last chapter.

                    *   *   *

Very early in the poem the Pardoner comes on the scene. Long before the famous act where Piers rejects a bull of Indulgence (B VII), the official who went round offering this kind of document is presented in a lifelike way which in modernized English reads as follows:

> A pardoner preached as though he were a priest. He brought out a document with a bishop's seals, and said that he himself might absolve all the people of breaking the fast and broken promises. Unlearned men believed him easily and fell for these words. They came up and knelt to kiss the document while he dazzled them with his authorization and bleared their eyes and raked in their rings and brooches with his stereotyped bit of parchment.

It is clear this fraudster is in conspiracy with the parish priest whose pulpit he is allowed to use. Only later do we get some notion of what was being offered. Here the emphasis is on the salesmanship, just as in Chaucer's vignette of the same offer in the *Canterbury Tales*:

'Kneel', he said, 'and receive my pardon, or for that matter take it with you as you go

> Or elles taketh pardoun as ye wende,
> Al newe and fressh at every miles end,
> So that ye offren, alwey newe and newe,
> Nobles or pens . . .'   (CT VI 920)

What, of course, the parishioners wanted for their rings and brooches, nobles and pence, was some form of the same mixture everybody wants and believers pray for – 'spiritual and temporal benefits', as they say or, in

---

[13] Richard H. and Mary A. Rouse, 'The Franciscans and Books: Lollard accusations and the Franciscan response', in *From Ockham to Wyclif*, ed. Anne Hudson and Michael Wilks (Studies in Church History, Subsidia 5. Ecclesiastical History Society, 1987), pp. 369–84.

individualized terms, mercy for things done wrong, a good harvest, a return to health of someone sick, a happy family.[14] There was no sharp division between moral good and physical good, since the middle ages followed the Lord's own injunctions to ask for both; only some later consciences recoil at the earthy petitions of humankind. The irony of the fourteenth century was directed rather at those who expected benefits automatically and without any reflection at all upon a Father who was asked, in other words, a sale. That was the essence of magic, the sin of Simon Magus (Acts 8).

None of this makes full sense without a historical glance backward at developments in the ideas of penance and punishment.

In the early centuries of Christianity people thought of baptism as the great unrepeatable act of cleansing which opened to the new convert a kingdom of heaven believed to be in some way imminent. This was new and special to Christianity, not like the ceremonial washings of the Jews (and later of Muslims) which, accompanied by prayers, had the regular reconciliatory character of contrition. The first Christians seem to have been so impressed by the teaching on baptism that they hardly knew how to deal with their own sinners. Backsliding into serious sin was visited with draconian public penances and exclusion from the Christian community until they had been performed.

The idea that sin incurred a debt which had to be exactly paid was deeply ingrained. Régimes of fasting and discipline over long periods were imposed, and reconciliation allowed only after the stages of contrition, confession and satisfaction had been completed. One mode of satisfaction was to visit Jerusalem where the Redeemer had suffered, and this became the principal pilgrimage.[15] St Jerome (347–419), who had settled there to study, observed rather tartly that it was not seeing Jerusalem that was praiseworthy but living a good life there, which was a viewpoint much like Langland's a thousand years later.

Before long, penances became abbreviated and might be performed after the sinner had been reconciled to the church by confession. The Jerusalem pilgrimage remained a way of paying a serious sinner's debt to God, and when the Crusades began and the journey became a sort of armed pilgrimage, the pope offered remission of the punishment due to sin for those who took part.

Slowly the theologians distinguished between the guilt of sin, which was taken away by contrition and confession, and the punishment due, which was paid for by some sort of suffering, either during life in the world or 'in purgatory' after death. Purgatory, as the word implies, was said to be a state

---

[14] The Pardoner's Prologue. See also Geoffrey Shepherd, 'Religion and Philosophy in Chaucer', in Derek Brewer (ed.) *Geoffrey Chaucer: Writers and their Background* (1974, reprinted 1990), pp. 262–89.

[15] For an excellent account of early indulgences, see H. E. Mayer, *The Crusades* (Engl. transl. Oxford, 1972), pp. 26ff.

in which souls destined for eternal happiness in God's heaven (and therefore 'holy') were purified of the deformities left by sins already forgiven.

Though the temporary nature of this purgatory would seem by definition to involve a time-scale of human existence after death, the later application of precise periods of indulgence – forty days, for instance – had reference not to a mysteriously measured sojourn in Purgatory, but to the amount of remission which would have been earned by so many days canonical penance in the early church.

It seems hardly surprising that matters as abstruse as these should be liable to misunderstanding, quite apart from rich opportunities to abuse them. But in fairness to the draughtsmen of papal and conciliar texts, the doctrine was never basically altered. Whatever our views on 2 Maccabees 12:42–5 and 1 Corinthians 3:15, texts used to support the doctrine of purgatory, the church decided that contrite sinners might be treated indulgently, by lightening the payment of the spiritual debts they owed. Indulgence and pardon came to mean much the same thing, just as in forgiving a friend's injury to us we might say we had treated him with indulgence. But whereas our forgiveness could ideally go out to someone who was not really sorry for what he had done, theologians could not presume to say this of God, and it was held that pardon of the guilt itself (*culpa*) was impossible unless the penitent desired it by regretting the sin. This regret was usually called remorse or repentance. It was possible to be repentant out of pure love of God (contrition) or out of fear of punishment (attrition). Either allowed God to forgive you; and despite all the seas of metaphorical tears shed by writers, repentance was and is a mental act not an emotional one. Sincerely made, the debt due (*pena*) could then be paid.

Interestingly, a fully developed doctrine of 'Indulgences' arrived on the scene about the time of Langland himself, who muttered that it had to be believed but was very dangerous. It was in 1343 that Pope Clement VI declared in his bull *Unigenitus* that St Peter and his papal successors might draw upon the heavenly treasury of Christ's merits and grant out from it the partial or total remission of the temporal punishment for sin to those who were truly penitent and had been to confession.[16]

In the twentieth century these ideas often seem crude or grotesque. Divine retribution, the exact measurability of blame, and for that matter personal immortality are obviously questioned. But it would be unhistorical to represent even late medieval indulgences as officially materialistic nego-tiations with God, because there was always the unknown quality: the inner dispositions of the penitent. Even a full remission of punishment (a 'plenary indulgence') could only amount to the equivalent of what the penitent could possibly have received after a full canonical penance as in the early days of church discipline. No one, not even the offender, can be certain what it is to

[16] Denziger, *Enchiridion Symbolorum* (Herder, ed. of 1948), paras. 550–2.

PLATE 1. 'The Lord is the portion of my inheritance' (Ps. 15:5, Vulgate numbering), recited at the moment of the first tonsure, which conferred the clerical state and signified supposed ability to read Scripture. (Cf. B XII esp. 187–9)

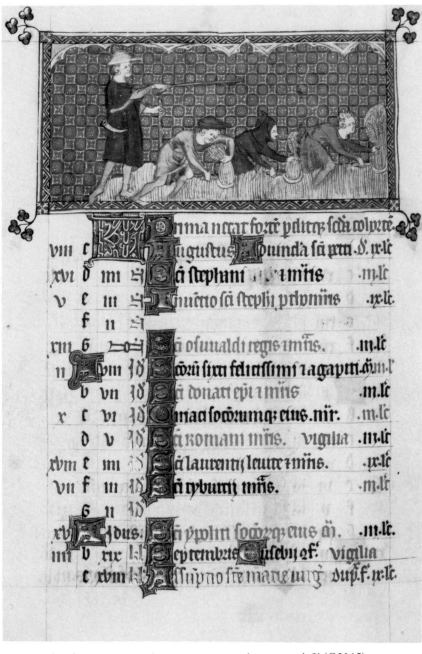

PLATE 2. 'Can you reap or be a reap-reeve and get up early?' (C V 15)

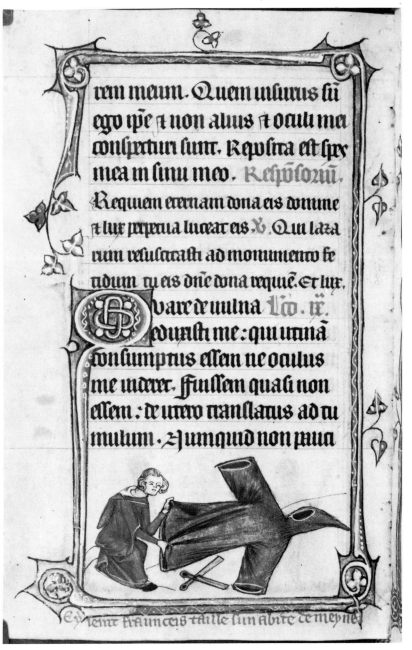

rem meum. Quem uisurus su
ego ipe ꝗ non alius ꝗ oculi mei
conspecturi sunt. Reposita est spes
mea in sinu meo. Responsorium.

Requiem eternam dona eis domine
ꝗ lux perpetua luceat eis ℣. Qui laza
rum resuscitasti ad monumentum fe
tidum tu eis domine dona requiem. Et lux.

uare de uulna Lectio. ix.
eduxisti me: qui utinam
consumptus essem ne oculus
me uideret. fuissem quasi non
essem: de utero translatus ad tu
mulum. Numquid non paucitas

Ecce uenit franceis taille sun abite ce meyne

PLATE 3. 'Pursuers of perfection should follow those like Dominic and
Francis who taught them how to live on little . . .' (B XV 415–21)

PLATE 4. '. . . and some chose trade, they prospered better, as it seems in the world's eyes . . .' (B Prol. 31–2)

PLATE 5. 'I have good ale. Will you try it, Glutton?' (B V 303)

PLATE 6. 'Now I am old and grey and have enough to live on I am going with the others on a pilgrimage, to do penance.'
(B VI 83–4)

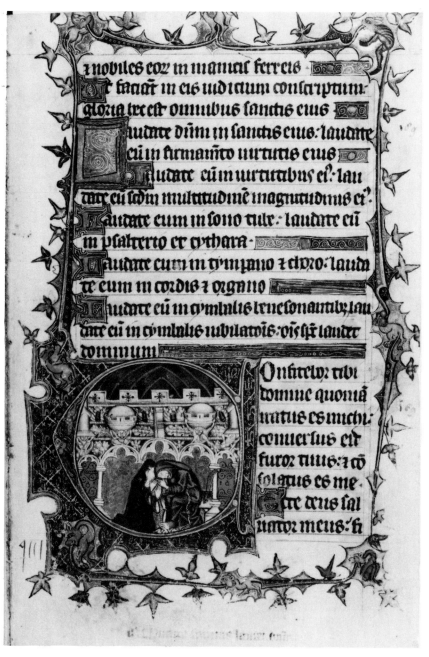

PLATE 7. 'Now repent, and never again give away secrets by your words or expression . . .' (B V 180–1)

PLATE 8. 'Go, confess to some friar: he'll love you if you're rich . . .' (B XI 54–5)

PLATE 9. 'If the bishop were holy and worth both his ears, his seal should not be sent out to deceive the people . . .' (B Prol. 78–9)

PLATE 10. '. . . by assent of themselves, as the two might agree, thus was wedlock wrought, and God himself it made . . .' (B IX 16–17)

be 'truly penitent' (*vere poenitens* in the phrase of the bull). Weeping can only be a figure of speech, an emotional reaction, or an attempted demonstration. And everyone knows that human beings differ vastly in sensitivity of conscience, ranging from amorality to obsessive scruples.

To tread a path of commonsense goodness over the years would seem the best aim, and it was this that Langland described in his own language when he asserted 'to trust on triennials is not so secure as is Dowel' (B VII 180–1), meaning that practical love is better than a month's worth of mechanical Masses.

In this way, the Pardons or Indulgences made familiar by Langland and Chaucer were historical developments from the dearly-bought hopes that proper penance had been done to the small placatory gestures of men and women leading uninterrupted private lives.

But turning to the Pardoner of Langland and Chaucer there is clearly yet more explaining to do. Good faith aside, there are material as well as spiritual benefits on offer. A local trade has developed where once such graces were to be acquired only by far travel and rigorous supplication. What has happened?

Let us for a moment reconsider the acts of penance. First we can see sinners journeying to Jerusalem to set straight their accounts with the Saviour, though we have to guess that most of them were very bad or very rich. What do they do when they get there? Surely they gaze on the sacred places, the gardens and the hills of the Gospel where signs had been given and the Passion enacted long ago, and the teaching given how to pray. So they pray, in some fashion – and perhaps devout residents begin to suggest touchings of landmarks and the treasuring of fragments said to be connected with Christ, relics of one sort or another which might be taken home.

Later, pilgrimages multiply and draw people also to Rome or Compostella or some other place made sacred by apostles. Later still, when the abbreviation of penances was well established, other shrines offered themselves, dozens within England itself.

But the pilgrimage in expiation of sin may also reverse itself. The sacred shrine may actually come to the sinner in the form of some relic duly authenticated, and sinners may await these, venerate them in costly display cabinets within easy reach or even – if the sinner is noble and rich – seek them for his own acquisition. Royal collectors of relics made abbeys famous; but the principle is the same for the goodman who rises before dawn to drink the water from a pardoner-blessed well. Just as a pilgrimage to some shrine with its relic or association could be made an indulgenced work, so too could the veneration with prescribed prayers of a relic that had been transported to the village locality.

The last stage is the multiplication of holy pictures which receive ecclesiastical approval. These too could be indulgenced and the penitent might perform before them exactly the same acts of reverence stimulated in Jerusalem or Rome. Here is a recommendation from the great German preacher, Geiler von Kaisersberg, from a fifteenth-century pulpit:[17]

> If you cannot read, then take a picture of paper where Mary and Elizabeth are depicted as they meet each other – you buy it for a penny. Look at it and think how happy they had been, and of good things . . . Thereafter show yourself to them in an outer reverence, kiss the image on the paper, bow in front of the image, kneel before it . . .

This brings us back to the pardoner as the purveyor of indulgences, for he could indeed be in a position to offer two kinds of bargain. He could preach remission of penance to all truly confessed people who contributed to a specified object, like a hospital for the poor; and he might also produce some relic for veneration with specific prayers. Chaucer makes play with the latter. Langland is concerned rather with the pardon itself and refers to the pope's sealed letters of authentication.

But the two are brought together in the canon law made at the General Council of 1215[18] which said that an established relic must only be shown to the public in a reliquary, and new relics only with papal approval. Too often, it continued, pilgrims are deceived by lies and false documents. The preaching of a veneration or of an appeal for alms may only be made by holders of a licence from pope or bishop. Furthermore, these collectors of alms must be modest and discreet; they must not stay in taverns or incur high costs, nor wear the habit of some imaginary religious order. They must not grant excessive and indiscreet indulgences and thereby lessen the satisfaction required at the sacrament of penance.

The pardoner therefore had need of one critical document: his letter of authority from pope or bishop. English bishops of Langland's time and afterwards were always complaining about false collectors who canvassed for poor hospitals or offered spurious indulgences, and they insisted that would-be preachers produce on demand a bishop's special permission sealed on the back with his signet.[19]

Of course there were plenty of genuine ones. For example, in 1360 the bishop of Coventry and Lichfield wrote on behalf of a representative of St Botulph's priory, Colchester, who was preaching for their building-fund with the help of papal indulgences, and sped him on his way by ordering all

---

[17] Sixten Ringbom, *Icon to Narrative: the rise of the dramatic close-up in fifteenth-century devotional painting* (Åbo, Finland, 1965), ch. 1.

[18] C.-J. Hefele and H. Leclercq, *Histoire des Conciles*, vol. V part 2 (Paris, 1913), pp. 1381–3; IV Lat. c. 62.

[19] *The Register of Robert Hallum, bishop of Salisbury, 1407–17* (Canterbury and York Society, 1982), No. 871.

other appeals to be suspended during the tour.[20] Then again, Simon Langham, who was archbishop of Canterbury (1366–68) about the time Langland was finishing his A-text, granted a forty-day indulgence for a whole series of good causes: success of the English armies, remission of the plague and recovery of the sick, repair to Stratford-on-Avon bridge, the support of hospitals at Hythe, Seaford, Charing Cross (St Mary Rouncey) and Rome; also for the support of an anchorite and his fellow (*socius*) whose enclosure in the churchyard of St Lawrence Jewry, London, had just been consecrated.[21]

Such news-items could hardly have escaped Langland's notice, but his concern was not the detail of good works but the pardon itself. 'I never had a thing from the pope', he made Haukyn say, 'Save a pardon with a peis of leed and two polles amyddes!' (B XIII 246). [Except a pardon sealed with a piece of lead impressed in the middle with two heads, i.e. of SS Peter and Paul.]

So Truth who had offered the pardon earlier in the poem had in fact been properly furnished with the papal letters duly sealed with the leaden *bulla* such as was used in routine matters by the papal chancery. Piers, in rejecting it, was not questioning its authenticity, which the poet rather grudgingly admitted (B VIII 174f.), but was declaring his belief in the absolute need for the penitent's right intention, expressed poetically as 'Do Well' in the pilgrimage of daily life.

*   *   *

In London Langland lived in the midst of ecclesiastical life at its most institutional. Many English bishops had town-houses there, and their households were staffed with clerks and chaplains. The Cathedral was served by an army of clergy from the Dean and Chapter down to vicars-choral and official scribes, the equivalent of today's secretarial staff. Then there were the monasteries, great and small, for men or women, and the chaplains of at least a hundred parish churches. At times when Parliament met, so normally did Canterbury Convocation which brought bishops and clergy, high and low, with all their attendants, from distant parts of England. So when Langland was probably living in London we have to think of scores of extra clergy streaming in every two years or so.

These tides of men in clerical garb, some plain, some in silk and fur, flowed through the City bringing trade to suppliers and doubtless alms to the poor. Many of the clergy that London would be likely to see came from affluent society and had money to pay for cloth, foods, wines, fodder, parchment and a dozen forms of service.

---

[20] *The Second Register of Bishop Robert de Stretton, 1360–85*, ed. R. A. Wilson (William Salt Archaeological Society, 1905), p. 91.
[21] *The Register of Simon Langham, archbishop of Canterbury [1366–8]*, ed. A. C. Wood (Canterbury and York Society, 1956), pp. 130–1, 151–2, 192–3.

A more permanent fixture were the church courts, staffed with graduate clergy and populated week in week out by people with all kinds of law-suit or else accused of one of the clerically judged offences. The city was thick with ecclesiastical lawyers. A quick run-through will convey some idea of the place law could occupy in religious matters, and one can think of no modern parallel except Rome. But unlike Rome, medieval London was not centralized but indeed almost chaotic in its handling of those areas of life where the spirit and the law have to meet.

First there was the archbishop of Canterbury who had a regular court mainly hearing appeals from all over England south of Yorkshire and including Wales. This was the 'Court of the Arches' held in the church of St Mary-le-Bow. Its regular staff were highly qualified in Canon and Civil law (the law of the Church and the Roman law). Some of them would become bishops, all had enviable incomes. They could well stand for the Simony and Civil who are shown as Counsel to Lady Meed (B II 63 etc.). The archbishop also had more personal courts at Lambeth, his London palace.

But London was mostly the judicial territory of its own bishop, who had a regular court (bishops' courts are generally called Consistory Courts), and this sat once or twice a week in the Long Chapel of St Paul's Cathedral, hearing cases which came from all over the London diocese; this covered much of Middlesex and Essex as well as London itself.[22] Like all courts it had a large staff to represent the parties, ask endless questions, get the people to court, and publish judgments by sending out letters to everyone involved. Being Roman, everything was written down, of course in Latin.

Courts like these had jurisdiction over all matters to do with marriage, wills, church property like tithes and benefices, the behaviour of clerks and the morals of everyone.

To take ordinary lay people alone, they might find themselves in court because of a dispute about a marriage or inheritance problem and also what we would call contract, since breach of contract could be regarded as breaking a promise and therefore perjury and therefore enforceable by church law. Layfolk could also be prosecuted by the church court itself for things like sexual offences, slanderous behaviour and Sunday trading. These were the common matters. More dramatic cases like sorcery were uncommon, and heresy appeared rarely in England before the spread of Lollardy from the end of the fourteenth century. At the other end of the scale, the courts seem to have bothered little about irregular attendance at church or domestic brawls. There was quite enough business in trying to do roughly what a modern magistrate's court might do. The courts were public tribunals, not confessionals.

---

[22] For a clear summary account, see Richard M. Wunderli, *London Church Courts and Society on the eve of the Reformation* (Medieval Academy of America, Cambridge, Mass., 1981).

They were also businesses, slow and expensive, and as in all ages most used by those with big money, scarring injustice or an uncertain grasp on reality.

But these bishop's courts were not the whole story. There were also the intermeshing jurisdictions of other ecclesiastics, some of them rather strange.

A diocese was divided up into archdeaconries, and every archdeacon had a court. This too was a business as well as a tribunal, and the efficient archdeacon a local manager. 'The purse is the archdeacon's hell', commented Chaucer.

For London there were no fewer than four archdeaconry courts – for Middlesex, Essex, Colchester and the city itself, and their main work was to supervise local morals and the many-sided work of the church-wardens. In addition, the Dean and Chapter of St Paul's had a jurisdiction over its own household-members, officials and tenants, and the archbishop of Canterbury had jurisdiction over thirteen London parishes where for ancient historical reasons he was patron.

There was also a monastic archdeacon of Westminster able by custom to hear cases among Westminster Abbey's tenants 'in matrimony and divorce'. It was a jurisdiction most annoying to other ecclesiastics because it was said to attract people with marriage-problems to go and live for a time in Westminster, get their judgments of divorce, and go home again. These judgments of 'nullity', as they are more correctly called, were themselves sometimes annulled as scandalous, and various attempts were made to expel Westminster agents from ordinary courts.[23]

These multiple courts flourished because there was an enormous case-load, and because the medieval world was a collection of households and jurisdictions, not a unitary state or church on the modern model. The notion that medieval Catholicism was somehow monolithic is erroneous. Apart from general assent to articles of the creed and norms of moral behaviour accepted with some variation in western Christendom, the medieval church existed like patchwork within patchwork: parishes within archdeaconries within dioceses within provinces. Within these at each level a profession of legally trained men operated in Latin the rules of books and the judgments of their reason above the babel of countless villagers.

There is also about the London church courts a startling co-existence of pomposity and irreverence. Learned bachelors in 'miniver mantle' laid down their Latin law hardly separated by the furniture from the jostling crowd of proctors, summoners, suitors, prostitutes and their friends.

A fifteenth-century ballad tells of a London boy called Jack who was charged with witchcraft by his cruel step-mother and her friend, Friar

[23] *The Register of Thomas Bourgchier, archbishop of Canterbury*, ed. F. R. H. Du Boulay (Canterbury and York Society, 1953), p. 91 and n.

Topias.[24] But the lad had a magic flute which bewitched all hearers to laugh and dance without control. The Official [president] took his seat and the crowd flocked to hear the cases – accusations against priests, wills to be proved, women taken in the wrong beds – until the friar and the step-mother were called. They present the boy and accuse him of this wickedness. 'Pipe up, Jack', says the Official, and at the first notes of the pipe the whole throng, proctors, priests, summoners and all, start prancing, unable to stop:

> Over the deske the Officiall ran,
> And hopt upon the table, then
> Straight jumpt unto the flore.
> The fryer that danct as fast as hee
> Mett him midway and dangerouslye
> Broke eithers face full sore . . .

When the summoners and the wenches who had come for their penances were well mingled on the floor, and the registrar had flattened others by swinging his inkhorn, order was restored and the case dismissed.

Langland's humour was less frivolous but not entirely absent. Church lawyers flit about his dream-world in a shadowy way. There seems a grim smile as his pen runs along the money-grubbing crowd round Lady Meed, purveyors and provisioners to great households, advocates from the Arches and the summoners who would be saddled up like hackneys to carry them:

> Forgoers and vitaillers and vokettes of the Arches
> I kan noght rekene the route that ran about Mede . . .
>
> (B II 61–2)

> [Suppliers and victuallers and advocates of the Court of Arches, I can't count the crowd that ran about Meed]

The distaste for lawyers of any sort who will open their mouths only for money was a fairly general sentiment, but the sharp point of protest at the church's jurisdiction was at its supposed distortion of matrimony, which Langland considered to be a special ill of his time.

In the middle of the poem Intelligence (*Wit*) lectures the dreamer about Conscience (*Inwit*) who inhabits the castle of the body, and the damage done if he is wrongly employed. The writer's views on regular, legitimate marriage, and his castigation of illegitimacy, are not specially remarkable (B IX 108–155); they are the teaching of any contemporary handbook for confessors. But suddenly he launches into an assault on disparate marriages for the sake of wealth. These 'uncomely couples', very unequal in age, produce no offspring but wretched quarrelling, the sound of which has become distressingly common:

[24] Wunderli, *op.cit.*, pp. 14–5.

In jelousie joyelees and janglynge on bedde,
Many a peire sithen the pestilence han plight hem togideres . . .
                                                    (B IX 166–7)

[In joyless jealousy and wrangling in bed, many a pair have got
married since the pestilence . . .]

At first sight the accusations look wild and scattered. He goes on immediately to lay down good conduct in sexual relations, which are of course
to be confined to marriage and limited to the times approved in the moral
handbooks. But at both the beginning and the end of *Piers Plowman* there
are short, powerful moments of hostility to adultery and divorce, disorders
the poet links closely with the goings-on in church courts.

The sense of matrimonial abuse so consistently conveyed throughout the
poem is striking, but if we look at his complaints together it may be possible
to get some idea why he wrote in that way.

In the first place, Langland was right about marriages between partners of
unequal ages, but wrong in supposing them a new development since the
plagues of the mid-fourteenth century. Throughout the medieval period and
before then and indeed since, marriage between individuals who had any
property at all was a property-contract, even though it may also have been a
union of lovers and a continuation of families. Religious thinkers who held
marriage to be a sacrament themselves recognized it was in fact a joining of
families as well as of the partners and formed occasion and opportunity for
widening friendships and nourishing new generations in legitimate enjoy-
ment of property.

Every age has its ways of introducing couples with a view to marriage, and
the medieval methods included the use of a middle or 'mean' person, who
might be an influential friend or the priest, but also could be a professional
broker, the ancestor of modern 'dating agencies'. Desirable though it always
is that the families should be pleased, in the middle ages it was normally
obligatory. But there is no reason to suppose normality meant riding
roughshod over personal preference. Surviving wills and letters on the
whole give a picture of introductions, agreements all round, and a sense too
that it was more than a civil contract:

And thus was wedlock ywroght with a mene persone –
First by the fadres wille and the frendes conseille,
And sithenes by assent of hemself, as thei two myghte acorde;
And thus was wedlock ywroght, and God hymself it made . . .
                                                    (B IX 114–7)

[And thus marriage was made through an intermediate person
but first according to the wish of the father and the advice of the
family and then by the agreement of the partners made in their
own way; and thus marriage was made and God himself provided
it.]

Langland was not exactly disapproving of the customs of his day, though he wrote warmly elsewhere of the girl who 'for a man's love' left her father's family without the services of a broker (B XIV 263–9). In any case Langland's central point is that any valid marriage is one that 'God himself made'.

Langland's strong objection was to professional intermediaries who operated for a profit without the true consent of the parties, and also to any betrothals arranged for the sake of property alone.

But what he condemned was not new. Mercenary marriages were as old as the hills, and not confined to any one level of society. In 1185 Henry II had a list made and kept in his Exchequer of all the ladies and boys whose marriages were in the king's gift, out of which he might make a profit in selling to a good bidder some partner with a rich inheritance. Down the scale of all those who held land in feudal tenure the custody of heirs and heiresses and the right to 'guide' their marriages was a lucrative business. This was still going on under Queen Elizabeth I.

London citizens were just as eager to advance themselves and their families by marriage. Heiresses, young or old, were objects of keen competition, and often they were widows with accumulated capital. A well-known story comes from 1484 but illustrates dramatically the sort of thing possible earlier.

A draper called George Bulstrode made a marriage-contract with a widow and spent three years during their betrothal building up her business; he sent her presents, but kept careful account of them. When he went abroad to Spain on business she turned to a rival, 'not fearing the damnation of her soul', as the London record says,[25] and when Bulstrode came home she refused to marry him and ultimately died without re-marrying at all. The case got into London City records because the thwarted draper sued for the return of his money on the grounds of broken contract.

Further down the social scale were some manorial communities belonging to the bishopric of Winchester. A study of their records from the thirteenth century, an age of overpopulation and land-hunger, has shown that on the more densely inhabited manors, like Taunton in Somerset, the marriage of young men with landed widows was a habitual way of acquiring a holding. On the woman's death the man often married a young girl, who in turn re-married when her much older spouse died. It was evidently not uncommon for such a woman to re-marry once or twice, and in this way any sons who might have succeeded to the holding could find themselves kept out by young step-mothers or youngish step-fathers. The historian who explained

[25] Sylvia Thrupp, *The Merchant Class of Medieval London* (Ann Arbor, 1948), p. 106.

this phenomenon, J. Z. Titow, borrowed the phrase 'marriage-fugue' to describe it.[26]

Medieval marriages were governed by two conditions which seem especially alien today, but which help to explain Langland's attitude, not because he was born out of his time but because he shared the developing and multiform Christian conscience of the fourteenth century and was supremely able to express himself in English.

These conditions were first the property-contractual element already described, and second the binding character of betrothal. There was a kind of tension between the two. That is to say, inheritance of property might depend on pleasing the family in marrying someone they wanted, but also for the marriage to be valid you had really to agree to it. And marriage started in a strong sense at betrothal.

Wills and letters from the middle ages refer to the power of parents and kinsfolk over the marriages of the young, especially daughters. There is a common phrase in the making of bequests: 'and I will that she be ruled in her marriage' by the surviving spouse or some influential friend or relation. A disobedient or headstrong child might forfeit her legacy or share. There is plenty of evidence that daughters did in fact sometimes stand up for their own choice. The strongest card in the hands of the eligible was the church's clear rule that a promise to marry created a bond, and that a proper promise could only be made if it were free, and by someone free to do so.

'The priest who married us' is a common but inaccurate phrase. The couple married each other, with priest as celebrant, master of ceremonies, and chief witness. But Roman and canon law requires at least two witnesses, and to be witnesses is one of the chief functions of wedding-guests. Above all this, the man and the woman had to be free and consenting, and these conditions were not met if either were acting under real duress, secret or open, nor, obviously, if one of them was already married, or too insane to know what was happening, and so on.

In medieval times as in modern, most marriages were straightforward. But there were clearly a considerable number where doubts or ambiguities existed, either at the time or later. There was no divorce law in the modern sense of ending a valid marriage and leaving the partners free to marry again. The Latin word *divortium* was used to mean a judgment of nullity, that no true marriage had taken place. No doubt many people in married distress searched about for ways of proving their marriages to have been invalid. Some also needed to confirm a satisfactory but legally disputed marriage.

Medieval matrimonial courts were busy not because people were more dishonest than they are now in employing lawyers to argue doubtful cases,

---

[26] J. Z. Titow, 'Some differences between manors and their effects on the conditions of the peasant in the thirteenth century', in *Agricultural History Review*, vol. 10 (1962), pp. 1–13.

nor because marriages were more unstable: that would be very hard to believe. A basic problem was the lack of documentation. There was as yet no system of parish registers. The clerical world had cumbersome methods of recording ordinations and various forms of licence relevant to its literate subjects. But the generality of layfolk could neither afford nor use routine written proofs of identity or status. Even people of property who needed to prove their age and relationship for inheritance purposes had to go before a royal official with roundabout oral and sworn testimony.

Now if this administrative immaturity is matched up with the subtleties of a clergy operating a 'mature' law in a matter as complex as marriage, it is plain there will be great scope for the courts to use their own judgment, both for good and ill. It is easy to be cynical. If a couple got a judgment the world could easily say, 'they could afford good lawyers' or alternatively, 'how cruel/unnecessary to make all that fuss'.

But there were real ambiguities to be solved, and a few types may be suggested as illustration.

> 'He said he would like to marry me and we slept together for months; was that a promise, and are we betrothed or even married?'
>
> 'He grew up in Norfolk and only came to these parts recently; he's a fine fellow and has asked me to marry him. Is he married already?'
>
> 'Almost everyone round here is related in some way: may I marry this man from the next village?'
>
> 'My uncle ill-treated me till I agreed to marry this rich man whom I cannot even like: did I really consent?'
>
> 'My first husband took ship to the Baltic seven years ago and no one has heard of him since, so now I am betrothed again: is this valid?'

Circumstances like these might lead a court to say that a couple were validly but irregularly married, or might create impediments to a marriage that had been or was yet to be celebrated. There were many facts to be looked at: relationship of the parties, possible pre-contracts, duress, state of mind, and so forth. If a serious impediment were proved by the sworn testimony of at least two credible witnesses, the judge might pronounce a *divortium*.

This brings us back for a moment to *Piers Plowman*. When Lady Meed was going to Westminster to decide whom she was to marry, she was formed up into a comical cavalcade of legal characters, including 'archdeacons and Officials and all their registrars' who were 'saddled with silver in order to permit our sins, such as adultery, divorces and secret usury . . .' (B II 174–6).[27]

---

[27] The passage continues with lines which have perplexed commentators:
    Paulynes Pryvees for pleintes in consistorie
    Shul serven myself that Cyvyle is nempned. (B II 177–8)
Its context is the subversion of the ecclesiastical courts of archdeacons' and

Much the same was said at the end of the poem, when Covetousness, who was subverting the law on all sides, rushed off to the Court of the Arches and bribed the Official to pronounce divorce on true wedlocks during the partners' lifetime:

> . . . he made lele matrymonye
> Departen er deeth cam, and a devors shapte . . .
>
> (B XX 138–39)

[He broke a valid marriage before the death of a partner, and fixed up a *divortium*].

Unfortunately we know rather little about actual English cases because so many records were lost, especially in the Great Fire of London in 1666. The argument of this chapter like the complaints of Langland are quite general. But they may be illustrated here by two actual documents.

The first is a pastoral letter sent by the archbishop of Canterbury from Lambeth Palace to be read to all the faithful at Paul's Cross and in parish churches.[28] It dates from 1455, but it is just one of a series of such warning letters about public abuses that go back many years.

The archbishop referred to long-standing complaints, especially from London, both about people who failed to get their wills properly witnessed, and about couples who got married without witnesses. The solemn Latin phrases would have required an explanation in English to congregations, but their message was the absolute need for at least two witnesses to prove any case in canon law. It claimed that a marriage properly promised between a free couple, even in complete privacy, was valid before God (however irregular the circumstances). But without witnesses it was easy for one or both parties in the future to change minds and make another marriage vow, thereby committing adultery and producing illegitimate children.

bishops' Officials so that they permitted adulteries, etc., which would therefore not be condemned by the bishop when he made his visitation. The word 'pryvee' was used of Meed when Holy Church said 'she was privy as I was in the pope's palace' (B II 23), meaning she lived and worked there. By analogy, *Paulynes pryvees* may well mean the ecclesiastical lawyers who worked in St Paul's, where the London church courts were regularly held. If so, the lines could be construed: 'the legal staff in St Paul's who deal with the pleas of the Consistory shall serve me, who am called Civil Law'. Canon Law was, of course, an outgrowth of the Civil Law, and its practitioners often qualified in both. In B II 109 'Piers the Pardoner of Paulynes doctrine' takes his place among the demonic legal witnesses to Meed's marriage-contract; I think he is, as a Pardoner, a useful butt as an official person recognizable as an unjust taker of money, like beadles, reeves and millers, and that Piers and Paulynes doctrine are for alliteration, the latter signifying the general support of church courts, esp. the Arches, for duly licensed indulgences.

28 *Register of Bourgchier* (as in n. 23), pp. 23–4, 92.

As a hoped-for remedy bishops were told to ensure the banns were called in churches and not dispense couples from this requirement as was often done in cases where people moved about from parish to parish.

The letter is reasonable historical evidence of conditions already described in these chapters. The population of England in general and London in particular had become more mobile since the plagues of mid-century. It was not only displaced manorial labourers who wandered about looking for work at better wages. People of almost every sort moved over the roads on business. The fiction of a pilgrimage to Canterbury joined by so varied a company was firmly rooted in possibility. But if the laws requiring labourers to carry a document saying where they had come from were quite unenforceable, it is not likely that a man who wanted to leave his wife could be tracked down easily.

The second documented case[29] shows a marriage tangle unravelled, but hardly with a happy ending.

In 1408 a man called William Roper of Hungerford in Wiltshire appeared before the Official of the Dean of Salisbury and denied he was truly married to Agnes on account of a pre-contract made with Alice Sawser.

Although he had been living with Agnes as her husband for two years, it seems that Alice had been pursuing him and had also got her brother to help her. At this stage William went back to Alice and got a *divortium* against Agnes, but Agnes was certainly not going to accept this. She got William summoned locally in Hungerford to answer a few more questions.

The case was heard in the parish church of Welford (Berkshire) before a trained canon lawyer (who also happened to be Treasurer of Lincoln Cathedral). Here Alice did her utmost to prove she was the true wife. She testified that William had said to her one Lent, 'Don't worry, Alice, I will always love you and never send you away.' A servant of William's had heard these words but could not swear they sounded like a promise. But Alice went on and insisted that William had said to her, 'I, William, take you as my wife, on account of the scandal which you have endured, being pregnant by me.' She said there were three witnesses of this but that two were now dead.

William was caught between the two women. He had shifted from one to the other, back again, and finally back again to Agnes. He said that Alice had forced the *divortium* on him, backed up by her brother. The unfortunate Alice could not produce two witnesses, and William declared he was married to Agnes.

The Official (ecclesiastical judge) had no option but to declare Agnes was the wife and imposed some penance on Alice.

It is not likely that this sad little history was specially complex or unusual. More difficult ones, or those where a lot of money was involved, tended to go on appeal to the Court of the Arches, or even to the papal court which would

---

[29] *Register of Hallum* (as in n. 19), No. 1128.

very likely refer it back to its own delegates in England. But there were numerous Alices and Agneses.

Langland might wave such lawsuits away, as ugly business, carried on for money. Yet these matters are hopelessly subjective. To hear a London proctor relaxing over wine and talking shop is one thing. To receive a story told in tears by a deserted woman is indeed another. The historian does not treat Langland as either judge or counsellor but is glad of evidence which may help explain the text.

Chapter 4

BEING TRUE AND DOING WELL

Although *Piers Plowman* is a complicated poem, it has a central message for readers today. It explains what one intelligent man six hundred years ago considered as the practice of Christianity, and it does so at just the moment when the English language was becoming generally understood both in speech and writing all over the country, but before the battle-lines were drawn between traditional religion and Lollard dissent.

Langland's achievement was remarkable both in its timing and his own uniqueness. There are many historical sources for fourteenth-century religion as an institution and as a community with an intellectual and devotional life. But little survives from the man in the street, and for all his singularity Langland was exactly that, 'roaming about' (B VIII 1), knocking at doors, and making verses to hold serious but not professional audiences.

This is not to call Langland typical, which would be absurd, nor simple, for he was complex to a degree. But his poem was about living in the world, mixing among people of various fortune, and seemingly directed to anyone who would listen. As entertainment it was full of diversions, and its division into sections suggests instalments and kept it spinning along.

People willing to read or listen to a text that survives in so many manuscripts cannot have failed to see that basically it was about the life of any one of them, under the form of a pilgrimage. The story was there, and it said so. The pilgrimage starts as a search for something called 'Truth', directed by a character called Piers who is reckoned to be more use to the newly fervent crowd than some tourist-pilgrim from Compostella or the like; and then the pilgrimage continues after abrupt changes as a search undertaken by the writer himself, real poet and fictitious dreamer, for 'Do Well', a goal both elusive and infinitely desirable.

This is the skeleton of the story, and if a short account can be given of what its author understood by 'Truth' and 'Do Well', then it would be possible to see a little more deeply what religion might mean in that age.

In modern English 'truth' is more frequently used to mean veracity, or factual accuracy, than faithful or honest behaviour. To praise a true patriot or whisper of true love are to use pleasant but rather old-fashioned expressions.

The fourteenth-century was more accustomed to the 'truth' which signified a fidelity to lords, friends, promises and so on. Chaucer himself wrote a little ballade (often called *Truth*) where the refrain promised him who would look beyond this world to heavenly things that '. . . truth thee shall deliver. . . .'[1] 'True men' likewise was a phrase heard about dissentients and sectaries,[2] whether among rebels in 1381 or a little later among and about the Lollards.

Langland lived before the meaning became loaded, yet belongs also to the world which was calling for all kinds of honesty in place of the trickeries and swindles said to be rampant. At the outset of *Piers Plowman* the dweller in the tower was named as Truth, 'father of faith' (B I 14) and the lady who came down to speak with Will told him to set his heart upon truth as the aim of his life's pilgrimage.

But from the beginning truth is presented as an option. Falsehood in the dark donjon could offer treasure too, the 'worship' of this world, obtainable but untrustworthy. 'Do not lead me to the treasure', the dreamer replies, 'but tell me how I may save my soul', and to this the famous answer is given

> Whan alle tresors arn tried . . . Treuthe is the beste   (B I 85)

and immediately defined as the possession of him

> Who is trewe of his tongue and telleth noon oother,
> And dooth the werkes therewith and wilneth no man ille
>
> (88–89)

> [who speaks nothing but the truth, and acts by it, wishing no man ill.]

The idea of truth involving both speaking and doing is taken up again when Do Well is described as a virtue followed by whomever 'is true of his tongue and of his two hands' (B VIII 81).

The recurrence of these lines in all three versions of the poem shows how the poet throughout his writing life joined the idea of truth both to tongue and hands, and as a practical man made no distinction between the way, the truth and the life.

Yet these are general words and do little more than establish that for Langland the practice of Christianity required the use of commonsense to

[1] F. N. Robinson (ed.), *The Works of Geoffrey Chaucer* (2nd edn 1966), pp. 536, 860–1.

[2] Anne Hudson, *Lollards and their Books* (1985), chapter 3.

discern the detailed workings of the world and some kind of intention to make choices.

Generalities easily drift away into platitudes, and more precise ideas are needed to understand the cast of Langland's thoughts. These are in fact provided through a close reading of the route-card invented by the writer for the journey to Truth. At his first appearance Piers finds the people looking for the way. They have asked a pilgrim covered with souvenir badges from the shrines of Christendom, but he has never heard of Saint Truth. But Piers Plowman has, and he volunteers instructions. It is these which give a clue to Langland's own understanding of Christianity (B V 533–629).

The ploughman describes the route to Truth's castle as a landscape over which a walker tramps and directs himself by landmarks, each noted in allegorical terms but set down with realistic features. To say briefly that the journey to Truth is by way of the Ten Commandments may be broadly correct, but it is the emphases and additions which count. They are overwhelmingly concerned with personal gentleness and the dispositions of a kindness one must suppose could not be taken for granted by the fourteenth-century observer. The lord of the castle is, to begin with, recommended not only as a good paymaster but one who 'always speaks to you kindly' (B V 553). The pilgrims, specified as men and women alike, are directed through 'meekness' and 'conscience', and to pass these is some kind of sign that the walker loves God and his neighbour and treats others as he would be treated himself. The stream next crossed is 'be gentle in speech', and after farms and hills designated as the usual commandments comes a wood of bribes 'hedged in with florins' (B V 581). It leads to 'speak the truth and mean it' and thus to the mansion roofed with love and the lowly speech of brothers.

A critic may retort that the passage is steeped in the imagery of the Wisdom Books of the Old Testament, and it would be surprising if Langland did not make his own the texts he knew so well, but at the end of his directions Piers is made to utter a powerful idea which informs the whole poem. It is that to enter the mansion is to find Truth dwelling in your heart; the image is embellished to suggest a locket dangling heart-shaped on a chain:

> Thow shalt see in thiselve Truthe sitte in thyn herte
> In a cheyne of charite . . .   (B V 606–7)

In this way the spiritual topography is established. The whole journey is into the heart, which is there all the time, and if the journey is made rightly, so then Truth is found there too, linked to the charity expressed in the daily words and acts of brotherly love.

By this time the story seemed to need a new start. Everybody had been told to look for Truth, and when the directions were given by Piers it turned out that truth was in the individual heart. A lot of time may be well employed in meditating that 'the kingdom of God is within you', but it doesn't make an obvious narrative. There is a call for action.

Langland managed the change-over in the crucial Pardon scene, where Truth sends a Pardon to Piers the Plowman and his heirs which should free from guilt and punishment all like him who work honestly (B VII). When a priest wants to read the pardon and the text is unfolded, all it says is 'Do well and have well and God shall have thy soul.' From this point the search is on, and in his visions the dreamer roams the world looking, asking, ruminating and possibly drawing nearer to Do Well. The hearer is swept along with curiosity to know what kind of a life it is that can almost be touched like a person.

This is to anticipate. The idea of 'Do Well' had been in the poem virtually from the beginning and seems to have been one of Langland's earliest images.

After the lady from the Tower had sketched the entire history of the world's creation and man's fall, she spelled out the connection between knowing and doing which pointed the poem on its way: 'those who do well as Holy Writ says and end up in truth, that is the best . . .' (B I 130–1).

An early problem was whether we can know how to do well. People cannot try to act 'well' if they cannot know what 'well' means. The poet timidly suggested his incapacity, and the lady gave him a sharp retort: 'you stupid fellow, your wits are dull. There is a natural knowledge in your heart which prompts you to love your Lord . . .' (B I 140f.)

This reproof leads directly on to the famous declaration on divine love – 'light as a linden leaf, piercing as a needle' (B I 156–7) – of which the intense lyricism won the passage a place in the *New Oxford Book of English Verse.*

Sceptics will not be convinced by lyricism, and the debate was alive in the fourteenth century as it is now, whether humankind can perceive and choose what is good. Langland himself was not trying to start an intellectual discussion or query the possibility of moral actions. He was assuming and asserting that you could so perceive, in order to get his Christian teaching going. In any case, he was less a philosopher than a man of simple affective piety. Those two types almost seem to share the late middle ages between them, but it is interesting that Langland could see the problem. His own basic theme was 'I know in my conscience what Christ will have me do' (C V 83).

To read through the text is to see that Do Well had for Langland a Scriptural rather than a philosophical origin. In the books of the prophets and in the psalms which were his daily fare the calls to amendment went out over Israel:

Cease to do evil and learn to do good   (Is. 1:16–17)

and

> Depart from evil and do good   (Ps. 34:14)

and as we have seen from the unfolded Pardon, the text written there was from the Athanasian Creed, itself a kind of psalm:[3] 'they who do good shall go into eternal life'. The root idea of Do Well is easy to find.

There is, however, a further problem. If the entry into eternal life could be gained through such simple and general instructions, and human beings had natural knowledge of how to go about such things, as seemed agreed, then we might well ask why Langland wrote at all.

In fact, he asked himself this question later on, when he was reproved again, this time by Imaginatif who said, 'you play about with versifying instead of saying your psalter. There are enough books to tell man what Do Well is . . .' (B XII 16–8).

Langland had thought about this too, and he gave two answers. In the first place, 'Truth' and 'Do Well' have to be taught: 'teach it to lewd men, for the lettered ones know it' (B I 136). In the second place, the books which were supposed to be so plentiful were insufficient for the real purpose he had in mind, and often misleading. As a consequence, the great poem which was Langland's 'solace' (B XII 22) was also regarded by him as work. It was a work of teaching he felt called to do. If it was really so easy to be told by anyone what Do Well was, then, he admitted explicitly, 'I would never go on with this work but simply go to church and tell my beads all day' (B XII 25–8).

And why were the books misleading? Was not Langland being rather arrogant about that? The answer was supplied by Imaginatif in the same passage, where he is immediately made by the author to say, 'there are books enough to tell men what Do Well is . . . and preachers to prove it, many a pair of friars' (B XII 17–19).

Everyone would know what Langland, like half the world, thought of the friars. 'Yes,' the sardonic thought seems to run, 'plenty of preachers: look at all these friars going about in their pairs with their sermons and arguments deceiving people.' Here then was an added reason for him to go on with his work, that he might speak of salvation in his verses not only to those who heard little but frivolity in their houses but also to those who in his view were being positively misled by clergy who should be instructing them, and were either too ignorant (like a lot of parish vicars) or too dishonest to tell them hard truths about virtue. We have to come back often to the anti-friar theme of *Piers Plowman*.

This is not quite all. Langland's desire to write about Do Well seemed to spring from an even more fundamental reason than a simple conviction that he could instruct others. His poem is not in itself a series of sermons but a discursive meditation. The reader has to say that in one way it is an account

---

[3] J. H. Newman, *A Grammar of Assent* (Uniform edition, 1870), p. 133.

of the writer's own inner life and in another way a richly-textured work of art in dialogue form which gave happiness to its creator. Both these achievements could emerge only from protracted reflections, by the hour, the month, the year. This is obvious from the text-history of the poem which, far from being a set of well-researched lectures, was a work of love that stirred his own self to inspect and improve.

Of course there were books to tell men what Do Well was, as Imaginatif argued in the dialogue. There were the Scriptures and other kinds of sacred writings, not least Augustine and Gregory whose texts abounded in one form or another for the edification of fourteenth-century literates. But other people's books were not the meditated life itself followed through labyrinths of trial and error, discouragements and shaky resolves, all recorded in himself before being put into literary shape for others. The literary shape is the fiction. But the experience used to make the poem cannot have been made up like the story of a novel. Langland's terrible earnestness is proof of his sincerity. Where he was right or wrong the reader judges for himself. But if the reader is a historian he should be safe in thinking he is learning something about a medieval man's understanding of Christianity.

* * *

When he began lecturing the Dreamer on his mode of life, Imaginatif made the point that if you decide, rightly, that the most saving virtue of all is charity, then St Paul was one of the great teachers (B XII 29–31; cf. I Cor. 13:13).

Of course this was the view of Langland, the creator of the text, and it looks as though he had begun quite early to form a religious consciousness framed round the idea of charity, which he memorably expressed in the triple phrase Do Well, Do Better and Do Best. If the Z version is in fact a prototype of the poem, he was already at the outset using the concept of Do Well: 'if Do Well does not help you, I wouldn't give a pie-crust for your pardon' (Z VIII 183).

Students of *Piers Plowman* have always been fascinated by the triple form and the ways in which Langland seems to have thought good, better and best as different from each other. It is not a rôle of this introductory book to discuss the 'three lives' in detail. But it is appropriate at least to suggest strongly that Langland was basically writing about the one life we each have. In Christian language this is the life of grace, lived by the practice of charity; however much people's lives differ in vocation, mode and even in the course of individual development, if a life is lived in charity and is therefore pleasing to God, then it derives from the single stock of grace:

> Right as a rose, that red is and swet,
> Out of a raggit rote and a rough brere
> Springeth and spredith, that spiceris desirith,

> Or as whete out of weed waxith, out of the erthe,
> So dobest out of dobet and dowel gyneth springe
> Among men of this molde that mek ben and kynde . . .
>   (A XII 123–8)

> [Just as a red, sweet rose springs and spreads out of a ragged root
> and rough briar to be plucked by perfumiers, or as wheat grows
> from among weeds out of the soil, so Do Best grows out of Do
> Better and Do Well among those men on this earth who are
> humble and kind of heart.]

The same idea is expressed exactly in Dame Study's parting words of
instruction to the Dreamer: 'if you want to find Do Well you must learn to
love truly, for Do Better and Do Best are both akin to charity' (B X 189–90).

Carried right through the poem, the three lives as stages in one life are
illustrated ultimately in the ministry of Christ himself. What one critic called
'a clever improvisation' signifies little more than the obvious, that Langland's view of Christianity was centred on the Gospel narrative and saw
clearly how the long-sought stages of charity are all to be found there. The
point is made in the poem quite briefly.

In the last Passus but one (B XIX), the poet takes time to explain how the
name of 'Christ' was added to 'Jesus' as he grew to manhood and undertook
his work as a conqueror. The dubious philology does not matter here; what
he wanted in short was to apportion his stages of Well, Better and Best to the
beginning, middle and end of Christ's public life.

At the marriage-feast of Cana when Jesus turned water into wine, 'there
bigan God of his grace to do wel . . .' (B XIX 110).

When later he healed, fed and comforted people wherever he went, then
he got a greater name, Do Better (128–9). Finally, after his death and
resurrection, Christ taught his apostles how to live the life of Do Best, or, as
the text itself puts it, recounting the story of Doubting Thomas and Christ's
blessing on all believers:

> And when this dede was doon, Dobest he thoughte,
> And yaf Piers power . . .   (B XIX 183–4; cf. Mt. 16:19; 28:19)

To make his point Langland manipulated the order of the Gospel texts,
but within eighty lines of his poem he created a neat *exemplum* of Christ's life
from the first, half-protesting, act of young manhood, through the heat and
burden of the day, to the ultimate commission to continue his work.

The trouble at this point is that a writer on the fourteenth century cannot
know how the fourteenth century received this little interpretation of
Christ's life. We cannot share the common stock of knowledge possessed by
Langland's contemporaries, and can only speak in probable and general
terms.

The act of Do Well was obviously one of hospitality at a family feast. There had been a muddle at Cana over the wine and the family were going to be shamed. The story was about this, not just a drinking party. The image of feasts is frequent in *Piers Plowman* and still in our own day has the power to warm us with thoughts of family celebrations, so that we can, as it were, enter our own lives through the poem.

At first sight the Do Better looks like care of the sick –

> He made lame to lepe and yaf light to blynde . . .   (125)

– but it is both more and less than that, because the Gospel healings and feedings were not surgical out-patients or soup-kitchens but signs of a personal love given to assembled crowds and individuals among them. The reader is free to interpret the miracles how he will, but the events were acts of charity: the five thousand got hungry again and the cured one day sickened again. Do Better therefore reads as an extension of family love to the wider world full of the poor, – the world as Langland knew it too.

Do Best, the most wide-ranging image of charity, is even more difficult to transmute because it is a wholly Christian *exemplum* and rests upon the idea of a personal faith. It is, however, plain to all who read the texts that Christ's commission was to teach all nations. So however one wishes to interpret it, Do Best is pictured as a universal activity.

In this way, the 'three lives' brought in again at the end of *Piers Plowman* and applied to Christ are like concentric circles radiating from a family feast, through a mission to the milling Near Eastern crowds, and out in an extending ripple of love to the whole world.

*   *   *

Three lives or one life, they belonged to charity, and for Langland who liked to think in precise detail this was a matter of loving your neighbour in ways which could be described.

In *Piers Plowman* the keenest test of charity is, paradoxically, the ability to notice charity in others. Langland wrote that charity sometimes dwells even in pilgrimages, but mainly in those which are made not to famous shrines but to poor men and prisoners, bringing them food. He had a special pity for the poor, but it was not, as with some Christians, a sentiment to exclude everybody else, for he held all people to be his blood brethren 'for God bought us all' (B VI 207). Charity could be anywhere. He is a good companion and has been seen in *both furs and russet*: 'I have seen him myself, sometimes in russet, and in fine pelts and costly furs and gilt trimmings' (C XVI 342–3).

The concrete detail makes *Piers Plowman* convincing both as a poem and as a meditation. We hear not only how men and women were dressed but also how they spoke and even how they looked at others. The gestures claim our attention.

In particular Langland makes use of three particular movements of the body which can signal inner feeling, both symbolically in the poem and, as everyone knows, in the actuality of our lives. They are the kiss, the feeling of a pulse, and the way of looking at someone.

The kiss may be either a seal of love or a cover for ill-will. It is taken by Langland from the psalms in his own way, as the kissing of mercy and truth, to signify joy at the redemption of those who had sat in darkness (B XVIII 422), and is followed closely in the text by the poet's cry to kneel to the cross and kiss it as a jewel. In the liturgy too the kiss of peace signifies the reconciliation between those who have left their gifts before the altar to resolve any quarrel they have had before sharing in the sacrifice (Mt. 5:23–24).

But the quarrel is not always resolved and may be nourished even through the acts of friendship. Envy provides an illustration from the poem:

> And when I meet him at market whom I most hate,
> I hail him genially as if I were his friend . . .   (B V 99–100)

and Langland goes on to show how the fourteenth century was no stranger to the Judas-gesture:

> The whiche tokne to this day is much yused,
> That is, kissynge and fair countenance and unkynde wille!
>   (B XVI 148–9)

The touch not of lips but of hand is a natural movement of considered help, whether in professional medicine, or in Christ's charismatic healing ('who touched my garments?', Mk. 5:30), or in the story of the Good Samaritan, image of charity in *Piers Plowman*, who stretched out his own hand to the wrist of the other to touch him and 'perceive by his pulse' that the injured man was in danger of dying (B XVII 68).

But it is the glancing eye which can convey the widest range of messages, since it can signal by indescribably minute movements a companion's dislike, or inattention, or love.

From Langland's understanding of human signals sprang his concern with seeing and seeming.[4] He referred more than once to friendly faces as signs of charity, and the blossoms on the Tree of Charity are expressly named as humble speech and 'benign looking' (B XVI 7). *Anima* who is made to speak at length about charity explains that the Christ-like Piers can see into men's hearts, and that there are some proud-hearted men who deceive their superiors by deferential looks yet 'to poor people have pepper in their nose'

---

[4] J. A. Burrow, 'Words, works and Will: theme and structure in *Piers Plowman*', in S. S. Hussey (ed.), *Critical Approaches* (1969), chapter 4.

(B XV 203). We might liken this to another kind of Judas betrayal, a 'false kiss of the eyes', so again Langland points to the eyes as windows of the soul:

> Ac the smoke and the smolder that smyt in oure eighen,
> That is coveitise and unkyndenesse . . .   (B XVIII 344–5)

> [But the smoke and fumes which get into our eyes are avarice and unkindness.]

This is the absolute reversal of the kind look, Langland's touchstone. For him the look is the easiest and swiftest imitation of Christ, who 'looks upon us in the likeness of poor men, searching us as we pass with looks of love, always seeking to know us by our kindness of heart and the way we cast our eyes . . .' (cf. B XI 184–7).

To sum up: Langland uses the expressions 'Truth' and 'Do Well' to teach the practical following of Christ. This was not expressed by him as doctrine, nor the sacraments, nor even as prayer, though he lived by all these, but in loving your neighbour, poor or rich, friend or foe. This you do by acts and looks of kindness. In Christian language this is called charity, and is the earthly expression of loving God.

To see more deeply Langland's understanding of charity we have to meet Piers the Plowman, subject of the next chapter.

Chapter 5

PIERS

William Langland was deep into his poem before he introduced the plough-man. Despite its recognized title of *Piers Plowman*, it must be remembered that Piers comes on to the scene late, and on only three main occasions. Furthermore, Piers undergoes changes between those occasions and some-times even within them. Guide, workman, overseer, contemplative, half-hidden preacher of love, Christ himself in human nature, and perhaps the angelic pope of medieval yearning: all these may be seen in him, though the poet never allows us plain certainty.

There are so many questions to be posed and hardly a single answer can be confidently given. We may even wonder whether Langland knew when he began what he was going to do later and whether, for all their compelling artistry, the transformations were entirely deliberate. But since Piers is the central mystery, and the object in the poem of a longing which does not end, we owe him some special attention.

The Vision had begun promisingly. The world's field full of folk had been presented, and for them the one universal treasure had been proposed: 'Truth is the best.' Lady Meed, embodiment of disproportionate wealth, had held the floor with the problem of her marriage-partner, Falsehood or Conscience. This vision had faded, replaced by that of Reason's sermon, that people should repent, confess, desire forgiveness and start to look for this Truth of which so much had been said.

They did not know how. The people were all milling about in a state of exaltation after their overdue confessions –

      'a thousent of men tho throngen to-geders'   (A V 260)

      [a thousand men there thronged together]

– but like a leaderless herd making a lot of noise and not knowing where to head.

Reason's stirring words were fresh in their minds, and especially the new shrine of unheard-of effectiveness which had been spoken of. 'All you people who go off to Compostella or the holy saints at Rome', Reason had said, '– you'd better take the road to St Truth, for he can save you all' (A V 40–1).

Everybody the crowd met got asked the way. Late in the afternoon they actually encountered a pilgrim covered in souvenir badges of his trips, and clustered round him as a man who really ought to know the route.

But the curt reply 'never heard of it' seems to have produced a disappointed silence, and as a new voice broke in, heads turned to look.

> 'Peter!' quod a plowman, and putte forth his hed
> (B V 537; cf. Z VI 13; A VI 28)

> ['By St Peter', said a ploughman, pushing his way through the crowd.]

Whether he was introducing himself through his namesake, or swearing mildly to attract attention, or even showing excitement at being able to help so many people, he none the less spoke his own name and took over the action.

All this occurs in the earliest known versions of the poem, so Piers Plowman must already have been a name with popular resonance, tripping off the tongue, at least by the 1360s and nearly a generation before the slogan-makers of the 1381 Revolt took it over for the good man who with John Trueman and all his fellows kept the world of work going.[1]

We cannot know if Langland invented it. There are very many examples from Scripture and the Fathers of ploughing as a figure of spiritual cultivation.[2] Though, as we saw in Chapter 2, the ploughman was one of a team, while the shepherd was more solitary, the shepherd with his flock is more usually a symbol of leadership while the plough turns the mind more naturally to the lonely furrow. Paradoxically, then, Piers Plowman works by himself, though always for others.

This does not mean he was without contacts. On the contrary, he could be everywhere or anywhere and to find him Conscience was at the last prepared to walk 'as wide as the world lasteth' (B XX 382). But at its beginning the poem moves briskly.

---

[1] T. Walsingham, *Historia Anglicana* ii, pp. 33–34 (Rolls Series 28, 1863–4), cited by Kenneth Sisam, *Fourteenth-century Verse and Prose* (ed. of 1970), pp. 160–1.

[2] Stephen A. Barney, 'The Plowshare of the Tongue: the progress of a symbol from the Bible to Piers Plowman', *Medieval Studies*, vol. 35 (Toronto 1973), pp. 261–93. If I understand the author's argument correctly, that Piers Plowman is a priest-like figure from his first appearance, I cannot wholeheartedly agree with it. Another valuable contribution in this context is Margaret Goldsmith's *The Figure of Piers Plowman: the image on the coin* (Cambridge: D. S. Brewer, 1981).

The ploughman declared he knew Truth as intimately as a clerk knew his books, and that many years earlier Conscience and Native Intelligence (Kynde Wit) had revealed to him Truth's dwelling-place and made him promise to serve Truth for ever.

Then the ploughman described his work, and this appeared to cover the whole business of keeping an estate going, from sowing seed to tailoring clothes, though oddly enough there is at first no allusion to ploughing.

But Piers – for his name is soon quite apparent – was chiefly concerned to convince the pilgrims what a good master-man relationship he enjoyed, with him giving satisfaction in every job that came along, and Truth paying prompt wages after each day's work, sometimes with a bonus (B V 537–52).

When the pilgrims wanted to know where to find this desirable situation of Truth, Piers was more than glad to direct them, and loud in his refusal of payment for the information.

By now the hearers would have found him a very strange ploughman, who did no ploughing, welcomed other workers as fellows and not as competitors, refused money, and was in addition available far from his work-place to give complex directions to all and sundry.

The narrative continues with sharpening contrast between the coarse actuality of the crowd – cutpurse, wafer-seller, pardoner and prostitute were there, cursing and wandering off – and the kind of transfigured idealism emanating from Piers. He sketches for them the long road to Truth's dwelling –

> a court as cler as the sonne   (B V 585)

– and explains in words with scriptural echoes the halls and chambers of the castle, vivid as the Tower of Truth and already recognizable as the human heart.

But the question of Piers's identity in this episode of his arrival is still not wholly clear, nor at first sight why Langland invented him. The vision had continued a long way without need of him, as the world and its people were being displayed to the audience, and it was only after Reason had preached and proposed not just repentance and confession but a long journey to Truth as satisfaction that the story's action took a new turn. For the pilgrims needed a guide, and the poet-dreamer could not be one because he was himself a traveller with untried equipment and defective directions. Although the tale was the teller's and the impulse to lead men was part of his own poetic vocation, it was inconceivable that he should start by knowing the way to Truth or Do Well, for the entire poem was his own voyage of discovery. So a guide was necessary, and that guide was Piers. The shift only came later, when Piers tore the Pardon and retired to pray, the crowd melted, and the dreamer-poet remained to search by himself.

When first Piers emerged from the crowd with his offer to show the way he was unmistakeably a man who worked with his hands. Even if his behaviour was not all of a piece, he was patently no priest or blessing-monger but a man none the less to whom people listened by force of his personal character and accumulated experience. Volunteering that he knew 'Truth' as well as a clerk knew his books, he established a professional authority even while declaring that his own knowledge was not itself bookish but a familiarity with whatever Truth was meant to stand for.

The directions he gave ran on consistently like those of a practical man: how to cross the drawbridge of prayer, to pass, in fact, the pillars of prayers to the saints, and how to call out the password at the right moment. ('I performed the penance the priest told me' was the password!) And so by wood-side and wicket-gate Piers took the listening crowd in imagination to the very presence of Truth, which they would find within themselves, first getting them to lend a hand on his half-acre before actually setting off.

However extraordinary the changes yet to be undergone by Piers Plowman, here in his first appearance he is perhaps at his most mysterious, almost as if his inventor were trying to make him out.

His solid manhood is unblemished, and though he arranges the precise tasks the people are to do, he is not one of them but removed from the human mixture of the crowd by a kind of formal perfection. He tells them the way to work – the women first – and indicates himself as the labourer who produces food in a world made secure by the faithful knight's protection. The wife credited to him is introduced simply as a hard worker who understands time's swift passing, and the children are models of an obedience to elders taught by the sharp slaps of paternalism.

Yet all the while Piers seems to be hovering between the vocation of labour and something more transcendental but not yet quite expressed. To the knight he says, 'I'll dress as a pilgrim and go with you . . . Just let me sow my corn and I'll turn to pilgrimage' (B VI 57–64). But to his family, who are not much consulted, he announces he has made his will and is about to set off.

Almost at once his life of ploughing appears to be an imminent reality and to stand for his pilgrimage, so that Piers seems for once to be a real ploughman and, indeed, as the team's leader, 'lord of the plough'.

During this short episode of field-work the details of Piers's humanity come alive. As the furrows are sliced and men hack away with spades Piers shouts masterfully, distributing praise and blame to those assigned work. Not everyone works well. He has problems of management and explodes with rage, appealing now to the knight, now to Hunger or, as we ourselves might say, to political and economic realities.

But Piers is not in complete control. He like all men is subservient to Hunger, whom he begs to go away. His management is tempered with compassion. 'Then had Piers pity on *all* poor people', the text says (C VIII 205), as he spoke of even the idlers as his blood-brethren, bought by God.

He too is prepared to learn with the other workers the lessons Hunger teaches, and to demonstrate in the lean time before harvest his own poor fare.

This image of working the land does not last very long, and Piers changes his role again before disappearing from the poem until Passus XIII. But before he makes his first exit Piers the plough-leader receives a communication. As the world's work goes on and people alternately surfeit and starve, the audience becomes aware that Truth has all the time been more than an abstraction, and in fact is a person who listens to what is going on:

> Treuthe herde telle herof . . .   (B VII 1f.)

is how the new section starts. 'Hearing tell' of how men and women labour at all their tasks, many of them having confessed with contrition, Truth approves the work they are doing and grants Piers a pardon from guilt and punishment, for him and his heirs for evermore.

With this dramatic leap forward the ploughman is identified – if any mistake had been possible – as the world's fundamental good worker whose labour earns him the kingdom of God. Piers is not here a disguised Christ. Divinity belongs to Truth, the awarder of pardon to the contrite. Nor is Piers here a papal figure, for the pope is referred to separately in the text as one who has some power of criticizing merchants and withholding full pardon from them; yet the merchants in fact receive some pardon through Piers for the charity they perform and are shown in the poem weeping for joy and 'praising Piers the Plowman for gaining them such an indulgence' (B VII 38).

So Piers is the labourer whose well doing earns him full relief from punishment and, more than that, one whose pardon spills over to earn something for others. And as Truth has made out the pardon to Piers *and his heirs for evermore*, all these heirs must represent similar honest labourers throughout the world's history. No others could earn so much, nor, of course, can we know how many there will be.

If Piers the good workman had stayed here, winning a living for the world, wasters and all, it would look like the end of the matter. But Langland's vision stretched further into the future, concentrating in his longing for his own Do Well.

The story is made to turn. Piers rejects the pardon, tearing it in anger (B version) or ignoring it (C version).

It is a twofold action. First, an ecclesiastical document is rejected by ripping across the parchment (anger doubtless lending the strength to tear the tough skin), but it is neither a rejection of the principle of pardons nor, even less, a rejection of the 'do well' text the document had been found to contain, and which activates it with spiritual validity (B VII 112). So Truth's pardon goes on in the transformed and proper dress of good life. Second, Piers the guide and good workman from that moment retires to a life of prayer and penance which, as he says, shall now be his plough (B VII 120), and leaves the whole stage to the poet-dreamer to make his long search for Do Well.

In other words, Piers stops being the one who accompanies people, and only reappears in the later phases as one who is himself sought after.

In reality, Piers and the dreamer are after the same thing, which is divine love, and we might even dare guess that the poet-dreamer in his heart desired that 'better part', that withdrawn life, in which, as he quotes, 'I have no food but tears day and night' (Ps. 41:4).

But the poet had his work to do in the world by his own apostolate of verse-making. With great skill he substitutes the Piers he has created for his own contemplative self. In the silence of 1500 lines Piers travels the hidden road of prayer and emerges transformed, teaching with authority and followed everywhere by the poet-dreamer on his long march.

The poet's road is not hidden. Along it he encounters all manner of human experiences appearing as actual people whose arguments leave him restless and unsatisfied. Not until he meets Patience, the first of the spiritual virtues, does he re-encounter Piers who now has something new and difficult, yet simple, to teach him.[3] It happens at a dinner-party.

Langland wrote two versions of this crucial passage which, though different, seem to re-enforce each other.

In the B version the dreamer is invited by Conscience to dine with a famous theologian. Scripture and Clergy are the guests, and Patience, who appears as a poor pilgrim begging a meal, is courteously asked in by Conscience.

The Doctor of Divinity enjoys himself hugely. In the place of honour (like the Pharisees with whom the friars were compared by their enemies), he eats and drinks well, and pontificates about Do Well. Then Clergy is asked by the host for his views, and comes into the conversation with some cryptic remarks about Piers Plowman. In effect he says that although there is an enormous amount of knowledge in the world, nevertheless there is a certain Piers Plowman who has taken to task people like the present learned company and shrugged aside all the sciences except love alone:

> For oon Piers the Plowman hath impugned us alle,
> And set alle sciences at a sop save love one . . . (B XIII 123–4)

Clergy, who represents sacred learning, then says something more about Piers's teaching which may seem difficult but which was quite appropriate in that learned setting and which is too important to pass over. After stressing

---

[3] For an illuminating discussion see J. F. Goodridge, *Piers the Ploughman*, translated into modern English with an introduction (Penguin Classics, edition of 1959), Appendix C: the riddle of Patience.

that Piers Plowman rests his whole teaching on texts about the love of God, Clergy quotes Piers as saying

> . . . that Dowel and Dobet arn two infinites,
> Whiche infinites with a feith fynden out Dobest,
> Which shal save mannes soule . . .   (B XIII 127–9)

> [. . . and he maintains that Do Well and Do Better are two infinites, which, by faith, discover Do Best; and that Do Best is the saviour of man's soul . . .]

This bit of conversation went on, '"I don't understand that," said Conscience, "but I know Piers well, and I can promise you he will say nothing which does not agree with Scripture. So let's leave this question till Piers comes and demonstrates all this in action."'

We saw in the previous chapter that Do Best was in the mind of Christ when he gave his universal commission to the apostles to go and teach all nations. Do Best is not different in kind from other actions pleasing to God, but in degree, in the sense that it is universal. Human beings who love God and neighbour in their limited daily lives are in their various ways doing well and even doing 'better' if they make special efforts or receive special graces. By calling these daily acts 'infinites', Langland seems to be saying that grace, or the love of God, cannot be quantified. 'Infinite' does not mean large or small but 'without boundaries'. Do Well is a life of love, not learning or knowledge, nor a series of stages marked up like a score at games. It may be on one day a remarkable act of generosity, on another day a single *paternoster*. All this reflects the mind of Langland, creator of Piers Plowman, who had agonized about the apparently different degrees of effort required to enter the kingdom of God. Now he is telling the world that these matters cannot really be measured anyway. People do the best they can, and God will do the rest.

In fact, this idea is developed in the same passage when Conscience says Piers will come and put it into action. Langland has already envisaged Christ in the guise of Piers who will freely offer his life for the whole world. Do Best is Christ's 'full, perfect and sufficient sacrifice', while Do Well and Do Better are the uncountable human acts of correspondence with Christ's sacrifice which are made by his believing followers and sweep them into the kingdom.

We have to remember that Langland was writing before Luther and even before the popular Lollards. There is nothing partisanly 'Catholic' or 'Protestant' about him. His faith is in Christ who asks only a contrite heart and then whatever the Christian can do, reasonably, but without boundaries.

If this part of the poem is obscure, it is probable Langland thought so too. In the C version it got altered, though it kept the same meaning.

The dinner-party takes place as before, and Patience is again the invited guest, but is now described as a poor man who came begging food for charity's sake, looking like Piers the Plowman and as if he were a pilgrim (C XV 33–5).

Patience and the poet-dreamer himself were put to sit at a side-table and served simple fare, namely, the 'sour loaf' and the drink of 'do penance' and 'long perseverance', which Patience received gratefully, though the dreamer couldn't take his scandalized eyes off the dais where the guest of honour, 'a man like a friar', was swilling and gobbling.

Conscience like a good host made efforts to direct the conversation. After the friar-theologian's self-confident views on Do Well and the rest, given correctly enough, between mouthfuls, Conscience turned to ask Clergy what he thought.

Perhaps he was disgusted at the doctor's manners. Anyway, Clergy answered shortly, and in effect said, 'Forgive me, but oughtn't we to keep these matters for the lecture-room? After all, Piers Plowman, that well-mannered pilgrim, has made all these subtleties look like nothing at all beside love and humility, . . . which are pretty difficult to find' (C XV 130–7).

It could have been an awkward moment. The theologian was a displeasing enough figure, and the rarity of humility was clearly a barb aimed at him. But he had not been wrong in his analysis of Do Well, save perhaps in emphasizing a little too much the important role of doctors in teaching it, and the greater kindness of friars to their sick brethren than to the poor. Clergy, standing as we know for sacred learning, had chosen to respond not so much with an argument as with a snub, brushing away intellectual talk and suggesting that the present company was unsuitable to discuss such matters. Between them all the conversation appears to have stopped in a tense silence.

At this point Piers Plowman, topic of the talk, suddenly materializes and himself speaks. For a brief moment he affirms the primacy of love. Using the motto to which Langland often recurs, 'the patient conquer', Piers announces that before God he himself will prove what he says, which is to love your enemies and do all you can to win their love too. 'And when he had spoken these words he vanished and no one knew where he had got to, so secretly he went' (from C XV 149–50).

The Passus continues to discuss patience in an involved sort of way, but the dinner-party had faded and Piers too had gone again, leaving more than ever a sense of his Christ-like nature – the hint of his coming demonstration of suffering's power to conquer, and the Gospel echo of his 'vanishing out of their sight' (e.g. Lk. 4:30; 24:31).

There is then a long interlude about the real meaning of poverty when Conscience and Patience work to convince Haukyn, who is perhaps the nearest the poem comes to describing a business-man (B XIV). Piers Plowman's third appearance, a long-drawn-out one, does not begin till the dreamer's own conversation with Anima (the soul) about the central topic of charity.

Those who come to *Piers Plowman* for the first time may quite likely find that it gets more difficult as it goes on, especially because it moves away from the busy scenes in the world and turns inward with increasing introspection. Nowhere is this more apparent than when we try to trace the person of Piers himself. To the present writer, the deep point is reached in the dialogue between the poet and the figure of Anima he had created to stand for the inner and essential person generally called the soul.

At the dinner-party Piers had been present with fleeting power to speak about charity, and this begins the difficult part, because charity is a rather embarrassing word to handle. To the casual twentieth-century reader it often means too little. It may signify giving money to a good cause. It may mean interpreting someone else's conduct as favourably as possible. But here it signifies the crucial Christian virtue and the one least well admired by those who are hostile to Christianity, since the lifelong intention to 'love' people, including enemies, seems to many a poor, unmanly kind of mentality.

But there it is. For St Paul the most dedicated acts of virtue were nothing unless, as he said, he had charity; and Christ himself defined it most precisely in the Gospel reports of his command to love one another.

The trouble is knowing it when we see it, in others and most of all in ourselves, for we are great self-deceivers. This is what Passus XV in the B text is about. For all his prejudices, Langland's psychology was good when he wrote about the discernment of charity, for he did not try to connect it specially with the rich or the poor. He spoke of haughty men who behave graciously and with patience towards their superiors 'and to poore people han pepir in the nose' (B XV 203). With equal penetration he described beggars and tramps who looked like saints, 'but more to get food easily than to seek perfection' (B XV 205–8).

What he wanted to say was that charity could not be recognized just by outward appearances, by what people said or did, and that priests themselves could easily be deceived. Only God can see into men's hearts, and that means Christ

> . . . no creature on earth
> But Piers the Plowman – *Petrus, id est*, Christus   (B XV 212)

So it seems that the secret is out, and that Piers is after all Christ himself.

The text, however, cannot be so easily interpreted as that. Piers has come through transformations, and will go through more, as Langland chose to manipulate his person for his own half-visible reasons. Here he wanted to make the statement which surely everyone needs to grasp in his own terms, that you cannot see, cannot know and cannot judge anyone else with safety. Clearly, for the daily purposes of law and behaviour we have recourse to evidence and make decisions. But there is no possibility of opening windows into men's souls.

For a Christian like Langland the difficulties are greater still, and to see this from the text requires us to leaf backwards a little through Passus XV.

'What is charity?' the poet had asked (B XV 149) '. . . where can you find a friend with so free a heart? I have lived all over the land, and men call me Long Will, but I have never yet found perfect charity . . . I have been told by theologians that Christ is everywhere; yet I have never seen him in person – only his reflection in myself, in as in a mirror (*in enigmate*) . . . and I should think the same is true of charity.'

This is the heart of the matter. The Christian knows both from Scripture and as a matter which is self-evident that 'no man has seen God at any time'. 'No man', Christ further said, 'Comes to the Father except by me.' This leaves human beings, believers included, at a sort of double remove. They cannot perceive God as he is, but at best, believing a man to be *capax Dei*, may perceive *that* he is. But even Christ in the humanity of the Gospels is no longer to be perceived walking and talking. So the one link of human perception which remains is of the men and women round us, including ourselves, fashioned in the image of God (Gen. 1:26).

This is what Langland was saying:

> 'Ac I seigh hym nevere soothly but as myself in a mirour . . .'
>
> (162)

Of course he could have pointed to some other person in his poem, but they are all fictive. Only in the mirror could he convey his actual perception of a man as an image of God. Even Piers – *id est Christus* – is not exactly and univocally the God who sees into hearts, but as Langland's supreme fiction is an image of the image of God.

That the God who hides himself should be reflected in human eyes was expressed centuries later, perhaps never better, by another English poet, Gerard Manly Hopkins:

> . . . Christ plays in ten thousand places,
> Lovely in limbs, and lovely in eyes not his . . .[4]

By now Langland was in the middle of his meditation about charity and its connection with Piers, and it seems as though he was so compelled by this

---

[4] G. M. Hopkins, 'As Kingfishers catch fire' (1882). The comparison had already been suggested by Elizabeth Salter, *Fourteenth-Century English Poetry: Contexts and Readings* (Oxford, 1983), p. 107. See also again the article by J. A. Burrow, cited above, Chapter 4 Note 4. On the reflection of faces in mirrors as images of the Lord, see 2 Cor. 3:17–18.

double image that he could not yet let it go. Later, when he came to write the C text, the author kept back Piers for a further while until the moment came to present him as an even more dramatically Christ-like figure riding towards his Passion. But the B text, with its restless and tumbling imagery, has more work in the meantime for Piers, and the reader should not ignore what the earlier version gives him.

It seemed as though Anima would never stop lamenting the decay of charity, and the voice continues on into Passus XVI. The hearers' minds had been led hither and thither over the detailed woes of Christendom, but now are allowed to rest in the shade of a great tree.

Not surprisingly, the tree was a pictorial and literary image more prominent in the middle ages even than in the nature-hungry industrial world. Reassuring as a symbol of life, its structure of roots, trunk, branches, leaves and fruit, can signify the birth through time of families and dynasties, the relationships of branches of knowledge and, with the alternate blessing and cursing of the fruitful and the barren trees, the mingling of good and bad, virtues and vices.

So now the audience is presented by Anima with the Tree of Charity. This was something everyone could visualize, and it was a short, artistic addition to place the roots of the tree in the human heart and have them tended by Piers. It is a counterpart to the incident far back in the poem when Truth, after much searching, was found to reside also in the human heart. We were then told Truth rested on a chain of charity. Now we are led forward to see that the human heart has a personal cultivator, and Anima produces with a flourish Piers as the landlord under whom Free Will hoes and weeds the soil: 'Piers the Plowman! I cried, and fainted with sheer joy on hearing his name' (B XVI 18–20).

I think we must not take too seriously the dreamer's fainting. 'Anoon I swouned after' seems a way of introducing another inner dream in which Piers can act. It was an involved manoeuvre, and was dropped in the C text. But it is too isolated a reaction to be more than that. It is not a prayer, much less an ecstasy brought on by the mere name of Piers, as though he were the object of a Jesus-prayer or other mantra popular in the fourteenth century. Certainly the sacralization of Piers continues in this Passus, but it is within an explanation of the whole history of redemption, not a personal devotion to a Piers-cum-Christ.

This Tree of Charity bears fruits which at one moment are pears and apples of wonderful sweetness, and at the next are human beings and 'the children of Piers Plowman'. The dreamer asks Piers to pick. The fruit cry and fall, and the Devil seizes the fallen ones and carries them off into the vestibule of hell. Piers in a rage takes up a tree-prop (the one said to signify Christ) and hits out at the Devil, determined to snatch back the fruit from him.

Piers is described on two important occasions in the poem as acting in sheer rage ('for pure tene'), and on both he is about to sacrifice himself to undo an evil. The first time was when he tore the pardon and vowed to consecrate his life to penance. The second is this moment when he resolves to rescue the fallen fruit from the Devil. The fruit are those who lived before the coming of Christ, good men and the children of Piers, and hence in the image of Piers. Among them are Abraham and Moses, who will be encountered again shortly. It is here another instance of Langland's anxiety, shared by contemporaries, about the fate of those who seemed by quirks of history and geography to have missed Christ's redemption.

*　　*　　*

Piers Plowman is a poem which seems to move like the sea. Vigorous actions and turbulent dialogue break like waves before giving place to stretches of reflection and teaching. So it is here. Piers is left in holy rage pursuing the Devil with a wooden prop while the poet yet once more recounts to his audience the life of Jesus from his conception to his death (B XVI 90–166).

It is natural to wonder why Langland should hold up the story's flow in this way to retell what his regular hearers had listened to before. Two reasons suggest themselves: first, that the way the poet rehearsed the Gospel story was designed especially to explain how good men and women of earlier ages would be redeemed 'in the fulness of time' because they are Piers's children; second, Langland was writing in sections which could be read as a serial, so a repetition of the central story would not bore an audience which might well have changed or lost the thread.

The story now moves forward as the poet awakes, rubs his eyes and looks all round him. He cannot see Piers, but as he stumbles to his feet to resume the search he encounters two other figures bent on the same quest. They are Abraham and Moses, and if the medieval readers did not know what was coming they would soon grasp that the charity which the poet had been talking about for so long was to be placed together with faith and hope, as it were in a triple gem-setting of theology.

For Abraham and Moses are symbols of faith and hope. Medieval literates knew that. In a typically subtle allusion Langland wrote how on mid-Lent Sunday he met a man 'as white as a hawthorn, and his name was Abraham' (B XVI 173). On that particular Sunday the epistle read at Mass was the story of Abraham and his son Isaac (Gal. 4:22–32) whose fidelity to Yahweh made Christians their true heirs. The old story in Genesis (chs. 12–22) made Abraham the first of the patriarchs, and of this his white hair is a symbol. He was taken up by the Christian scriptures as the very type of faith (cf. Jo. 8; Heb. 11:8).

So in these scenes Langland uses Biblical figures to demonstrate how faith and hope, known and served by the Jews, are buttresses to charity, the third and greatest of the virtues, specifically one of the New Testament and also of Langland's mental world. The first two are portrayed as historical human beings, but the third as the Good Samaritan of Christ's own parable, who dissolves in the poem into Piers and then into Christ himself.

This triad of faith, hope and charity, the so-called 'theological virtues', occurs throughout St Paul's letters but with greatest clarity in I Cor. 13, where the words have obviously been used for Langland's own images: 'Love never comes to an end . . . now we see only reflections in a mirror, mere riddles (*in enigmate*; cf. B XV 162), but then we shall be seeing face to face . . . As it is these remain, faith, hope and love; and the greatest of them is love.'

Some thought was needed, not least for Langland, to reconcile these Pauline virtues. His Abraham discourses on the Trinity and other hard, wordy concepts of the developed Christian faith. His Moses follows, personified as Hope –

> You have placed your hopes in Moses   (Jo. 5:45)

– who adds to Abraham's rather advanced lessons the requirements of the Law, which even as the simple Ten Commandments require a good deal of exposition. How complex all this is, we might think, following Langland, beside the heart's simplicity of love!

Indeed, Langland said it, not once but over and over, not brushing aside the more detailed matters required by men and women who can grasp them, but insisting on love's primacy. Long ago in the poem the verbiage of a church Pardon had been reduced to Do Well. Later the poet's own curiosity about 'all the subtle sciences' had been countered by the whisper at the dinner-party that 'one Piers Plowman had set all sciences at a sop save love alone'. Now, with daring reductionism, Moses opens the parchment of the Law to display neither Torah nor even Decalogue, but –

> Love God and love your neighbour . . . on these two commandments
> hang all the Law and the Prophets.

Of course Langland was not innovating but teaching the interior Christianity which superseded the detailed prescriptions of Judaism. He saw clearly that the Ten Commandments were concentrated in the Lord's 'new' one: 'love one another as I have loved you' (Jo. 13:34–5). On this hung all the Law and the Prophets (Lev. 19: 18).

Langland thought all this needed to be said not only because he saw a good deal of ignorance and malice, but because there seemed a real problem of placing belief and law-keeping, themselves good, in the perspective of charity.

'How can I tell which of you to believe?' cried the dreamer, bemused by Abraham with his theological lecture and by Hope who claimed to have discovered the Law but said nothing about the Trinity.

The argument about these complex teachings of Christianity lasted until the dreamer and his companions came upon the Samaritan riding to Jerusalem. It was a stroke of poetic brilliance to use the Good Samaritan, symbol of charity, the greatest of the virtues, as a way of explaining how simply faith and hope and all the creeds and laws were embodied and practised in the physical kindness of one social casualty to another: the despised Samaritan stretched out his hand to help a victim of robbery. It was an example of a charity that needed not to use many words, and in fact Langland cut short his Samaritan's speech: ' "no-one is ever so wretched that he cannot love others if he chooses . . . but I have stayed too long" ' . . . and he rode away like the wind' (from B XVII 347–53).

Piers was now near the end of the road. Glimpsed at the dinner-party in the person of Patience, spoken of as having eyes like those of Christ to discern charity, displaying to the dreamer the Tree of Charity itself, Piers moves in a chain of images to the Palm Sunday entry into Jerusalem.

Langland in this circuitous way arranges the transition from his own fictional creation of Piers Plowman to the historical Christ.

As the dreamer in his own poem he asked Faith, beside him in the window, if Piers was in this place, and Faith looked back at him, his eyes assenting.

'Jesus', he answered, 'in an act of chivalry will joust in Piers's coat of arms, wearing his helmet and mail, his human nature, so Christ will not be recognized here as God himself. He will be riding in Piers's doublet: no blow can wound him in his Godhead' (B XVIII 22–27).

At last the audience might expect the figures of Samaritan, Piers and Christ to merge in a single focus; but Langland declined even now to unify them. He had allowed just once the idea that charity can be known in the secret heart only by Piers the Plowman, Peter, 'that is Christ' (B XV 212), but he would go no farther. Piers remains this side of God, and in all his comings and goings he claims nothing but a kind of specialism in love.

The Passion was a historical act, known well enough in fourteenth-century England, and its drama, followed by the release of just souls from hell and the routing of devil and demons, is recounted with great power from scriptural and apocryphal sources without mention of Piers.

After the Passion, however, Piers comes on the scene again in a new stability of form. For just as the Passion was regarded as constantly re-enacted in the Mass, so Piers comes before the audience now like an icon, in hieratic posture, for Christ had suffered explicitly in Piers's vesture.

The seventh Vision in the B text finds the poet at Mass where he falls asleep and dreams

> That Piers the Plowman was peynted al blody,
> And com in with a cros bifore the comune peple,
> And right lik in alle lymes to Oure Lord Jesu . . .   (B XIX 6–8)

[. . . that Piers the Plowman, all stained with blood and bearing a cross, came in before the people. Yet in form and figure he looked exactly like Jesus.]

The entry is an ecclesiastical scene, enhanced by the poet's imagination which saw the leading crucifer indistinctly from the victim who himself is now priestly, vested and impassive, ceremoniously entering the sanctuary to re-enact for the millionth time his own sacrifice.

*   *   *

But Langland still had need of a special Piers. Writing in the late fourteenth century, and being the kind of man he was, Langland required someone different from a peaceful chaplain in an ordered world or a mystic silent in some cell.

Piers in fact receives the identity of his apostolic namesake Peter in order to continue the life of Christ on earth. The Holy Spirit descends upon Piers and his friends, and a long metaphor describes how Piers the Plowman is become manager of the whole estate of Grace, with all the beasts and equipment for gathering the harvest into the barn of Holy Church. 'Now is Piers to the plow . . .' (B XIX 337) are the summarising words which invest Piers with what is apparently his final function.

But in the end, who is he? The seminal text '*Thou art Peter*' (Mt. 16:18) offers one easy answer, that Piers should turn out to be Peter, principal apostle, an ideal pope, or the vicar of the Christ he had nearly become in the poem.

Yet the poem does not give us a wholly unambiguous message. Certainly Piers is for the moment dramatically identified with the Apostle Peter (B XIX 184). But in the same Passus he had already been identified with Christ in his human nature (12–14), and a few lines after the commission to St Peter Piers would again be named simply as Piers the Plowman (188).

The images are very compressed. It seems not unlikely that in this climax Langland intended to convey the idea that Christ, Piers and the ordinary good Christian, the heirs of Piers to whom Truth had once sent a pardon (B VII 24), participate in the lives of each other. Those who imitate Christ are said to become one with Christ (Jo. 14:20–23). Being heirs of Christ (Rom. 8:17) his followers also share in his priesthood, sometimes in the special apostolic way of receiving power to forgive sins and celebrate the Lord's Supper, and always in the general way in which all Christ's faithful share in his priesthood. Admittedly, this is a modern attempt to interpret an obscure Passus, and possibly Langland himself had not worked out the implications. He was not a theologian, let alone a modern one, and cannot be thought of as summarising any developed doctrine either of the priesthood of all believers or of the Petrine primacy. But it seems at least plain that Langland here in this late portion of his poem chose to merge the figures of Christ in his human nature, St Peter, and a Piers who is both ploughman and priest.

The founding of Holy Church in Passus XIX is represented as the building of Piers's barn in which, despite all dangers, it was intended that there should be peace, and supper celebrated of the bread of God's body, which grace through God's word gave Piers the power to make: 'Here is bread blessed, and God's body thereunder; Grace through the word of God gave Piers power to make it, and men are invited for their spiritual health to eat it once a month or as often as they have need, when they have paid their debts as Piers's pardon lays down' (from B XIX 388f.).

The reader must make up his or her own mind. Piers was Langland's poetic creation and in that sense was not anybody at all who can be infallibly identified. But we can be certain that Piers was always the soul's guide. The text says so at his very first appearance and never afterwards denies it.

Piers said he would do the guiding, and all the rest was a matter of following, up to the last lines where Conscience, voice of the poet, swore he would become a pilgrim

> And walken as wide as the world lasteth,
> To seken Piers the Plowman . . .   (B XX 382–3)

Chapter 6

THE LAST VISION

In some ways the ending of *Piers Plowman* is its most puzzling part, and open to widely different interpretations. The story had moved from its beginning in a confused world, through a life in which basic spiritual lessons were learned, to a triumphant climax in the Resurrection. Christ was victorious, the people who had sat in darkness had seen the great light, the Church had been built like a barn for the harvest of souls, and the mysterious Piers commissioned to run the whole estate of that Church as once he had directed his plough over half an acre.

But the moment Langland had written 'Now is Piers to the plow' (B XIX 337), all hell broke loose. The hosts of Antichrist assault the barn. To the very end the battle is renewed between the forces of good and evil. The good seem few and, led by Conscience, include Christians of whom the best were simple fools, 'mild and holy men who feared nothing that men could do to them' (B XX 65). The dreamer himself is reproached by a figure called Need for *not* being happy as an idle beggar.

The evil attackers, who inflicted wounds on Christians, were not only the deadly sins revived into violent action but, underpinning them, Antichrist himself who operated through guile and was able to make the sins themselves seem attractively good. A telling example was the camouflaging of the two great farm-horses, Confession and Contrition, so cleverly that even Conscience was confused, 'and businessmen did not know whether their profits were just or unjust' (B XIX 347–53).

The attack was not a simple destruction but a perversion from within, and as the poem draws to its end the more skilful agents of perversion appear as the friars who are presented in rapidly changing images: as not very good defenders of the barn, as flatterers for money, university philosophers in unlimited numbers, eager and easy confessors to parishioners who desert their own priests, and finally as Dr Friar Flatterer, the physician who attends Contrition and binds up his wounds with 'Private Subscription' till the patient falls asleep. 'He lies drowned in torpor', said Peace, 'and so do many others' –

The friar with his physic this folk hath enchanted (B XX 378–9)

However uncertain Langland's exact meanings, the last portion of his poem is full of interest and action and artistically consistent with what had gone before. It could have ended blandly with the founding of the Church. The fact that it didn't illustrate Langland's sense of history as continuing up to his own time and not completed once and for all where the Scriptures leave off.

But there are at least three ways of interpreting the end, and they are not necessarily quite distinct from each other. First, Langland may have believed in the imminence of the Last Days and ended his poem in this apocalyptic sense. Second, the poet may have been applying his Christian understanding to say that the struggle against evil on earth goes on, and that the evils he saw were powerful and threatening but not actually terminal. Third, he may have been writing in this last portion more agonizingly about himself as he became more aware of his own approaching end and his own loneliness and uncertainty. We may consider these possibilities in order.

Some scholars think that Langland expected the end of the world, heralded by 'Antichrist' and the attack of false prophets, as an imminent event. This view was put forward in a strongly-argued paper by Robert Adams,[1] who claimed to uncover in the last two *Passus* a cryptic teaching that the world was entering its final stage, when famine (*Nede*) and spiritual impoverishment would usher in the monster Leviathan, who is Satan, inhabiting the body of the last great Antichrist.

What this was supposed to mean in detail is obscure, but the argument runs that all medieval theologians were conscious in a general way of the Last Age round the corner, but that some individuals like Langland were convinced it was actually about to begin, and that Langland meant his dream that 'Antichrist came in man's form' (B XX 52–3) to be taken literally as an urgent prophecy.

According to this idea, Need was a sort of inverted John the Baptist, preparing the way for his false master, preaching the right to beg a living without regulation or trying to give anything in return on the ground that 'necessity knows no law', a text which occurs in the first Franciscan rule.[2] The mendicants were, of course, regarded as among the heralds of Antichrist. Such ideas, Robert Adams continued, are to be found in earlier writings used by Langland, such as Gregory the Great's *Commentary on Job* and the thirteenth-century anti-mendicant *Book of Antichrist*.

[1] Robert Adams, 'The Nature of Need in 'Piers Plowman', *Traditio* vol. 34 (1978), pp. 273–301.
[2] Penn R. Szittya, *The Antifraternal Tradition in Medieval Literature* (Princeton University Press, 1986), pp. 277–8.

A further idea in these writings was that patient and extreme poverty would be required to survive the imminent persecution, and it was for that reason Patience had told Haukyn he should not care about food and clothing but 'die as God wills whether of hunger or heat' (B XIV 57f.) Robert Adams pushed his view of Langland to the point where he saw in him a preacher of total poverty.

It is notoriously difficult to rebut arguments which claim that obscure texts contain secret teachings which only the worthy will recognize. Such texts tend to be self-fulfilling and baffle the reader without convincing him.

So it is here. However tempting it may be to read *Piers Plowman* as though it were an apocalyptic prophecy written, as Adams puts it, 'in a super-charged, expectant atmosphere', it is very hard for a historian to accept such an interpretation. Another one must be found.

In the first place, it is inherently improbable that a very long poem which is basically about the individual search for Christian love should be a vehicle for these excited alarms. Langland was a poet of perseverance, celebrating the habit of charity which is at the heart of Christian teaching. Following the example of Christ, Patience is made to tell Haukyn not to be solicitous about what he should eat or wear (B XIV 56–7; cf. Mt. 6:25–26); Haukyn was not being advised to starve himself.

If the poem itself as a whole does not read like a millenial manifesto, the same objection must be made on historical grounds. *Piers Plowman* was simply not written 'in a supercharged, expectant atmosphere' like that of the hot-house Paris lecture-rooms a hundred years earlier, where William of St Amour had revelled with other young masters in the imaginative exegesis of Scripture. To transfer that psychological climate to later fourteenth-century England seems a misreading of the age.

There were, as always, disturbances, but not popular expectation of the millenium. The plague which struck in 1348 appeared a scourge sent by God, and a leader of opinion like the monastic chronicler Thomas of Walsingham could write that 'the world could never be the same again'.[3] But the plagues recurred, and the many survivors often found conditions improved. Then when the Great Schism in the Latin Church began in 1378 the warring popes were accused of tearing the seamless robe of Christ, but not of heralding the last age. Three years later the Great Revolt terrified a lot of people; but it subsided, wages improved and serfdom gradually withered. In the writing-office of St Alban's abbey the chronicler conveyed a sense of routine in his comments on the passing seasons with which he prefaced his annual instal-ments of news: 'a year of dearth', or 'a fair and fruitful year'. In the parishes hundreds of testators continued to make bequests to their local churches and to the friars, asking that their souls be prayed for, often far into the future.

---

[3] Thomas Walsingham, *Historia Anglicana* (ed. H. T. Riley, Rolls Series, 1863–4), vol. I, pp. 277–8, 409.

The writings of solitaries and mystics which are still read today speak of eternity, but in voices of quiet counsel.

All these are marks of confidence that the world had a future. Political violence affected a minority, but there was nothing even in Richard II's England to compare with the extraordinary scenes of charismatic rebellion stirred up among the Hussites in central Europe half a century later.

A second and less extreme interpretation of Langland's last vision is therefore to read it as the struggle against evil which always continues. This is a commonplace in Christianity, and in other religions also. In some ages and to some people the struggle appears especially acute, and the text of *Piers Plowman* is more violent at the end than at the beginning.

But the final passages of the poem belong to its symmetry and are not uncharacteristic cries of despair. In many ways the end mirrors the beginning: Hunger afflicts an idle world at the start, pestilences carry off proud people at the end. Piers took pity on the first, Conscience prayed mercy for the second. Early and late, trees are overturned as a sign. The half-acre enlarges to the whole world, and in both Piers shows the way before disappearing.

So the world went on. Langland had made a drama out of the first Pentecost when Piers was given the gift of tongues, but the poet remained well aware how people forgot their repentances and needed the continued gifts of grace –

> For Antecrist and hise al the world shul greve
> And acombre thee, Conscience, but if Crist thee helpe . . .
> (B XIX 220–2)

> [For Antichrist and his followers will afflict the whole world and burden you, Conscience, unless Christ help you . . .]

Briefly put, Langland was not writing of the Last Times but of the search for grace and the effort that must be ever renewed till life's end (218). His own last words were of becoming a pilgrim and walking again, worldwide, in search of Piers.

If this second interpretation is better than the first, millenial, one, there is yet a third way of reading the end of *Piers Plowman*. This is not in itself contradictory but compatible with a Langland who envisaged no end but his own.

For the last vision (B XX 51ff.) is about the poet himself. It is reasonable to think that he saw the end of his poem and of his own life approaching: John But hinted as much in the lines added at the tail of an A-text MS:

> And whan this werk was wrought, ere Willie myghte a-spie,
> Deth delt him a dent . . .   (A XII 202–3)

[And when this work was done, before Will could turn round,
Death dealt him a blow.]

It is not that Langland changed the course of his argument. He maintained
a consistency through all the digressions in the pursuit of Do Well. But at the
end the emotion is heightened as the poet moves into the eighth and final
vision. His dream of Antichrist is not unlike the legends of how demons
besiege the bed of a dying man. The difference is that Langland remained
lucid to orchestrate his agony.

The poet began this last episode representing himself wide awake as he
meets the figure of Need.[4] Need is a hostile presence, not an interviewer who
was meant to be helpful like the others on the poet's journey. They met at
noon:

And it neghed neigh the noon, and with Nede I mette . . .

(B XX 4)

[It was nearly noon, and with Need I met.]

The hour gives a dramatic context, as so often in *Piers Plowman*, and 'noon'
at the centre of the line seems much more than an alliterative device. It
strikes a resonance, possibly intentional, with 'the scourge that wreaks
havoc at high noon' (Ps. 91:6), that is, the noonday devil (*demonium
meridianum*) dreaded by the Desert Fathers who had fought with spiritual
sloth in the deadly heat.

Certainly Need is a menacing apparition who mocks the dreamer for his
stupidity in not begging a living in return for nothing, since he was in need
and 'necessity knows no law'. Langland knew well enough that his living
came partly from alms, about which he felt half-guilty. He knew also (or he
would not have written it) that the text which justified begging in necessity
was a Franciscan one. Langland longed for a decent vocation, a living to earn
his bread, not a life 'in manner of a mendicant'. But Need continued to ply
him with the temptation not merely to beg but to feel humble in doing so,
and to imagine his likeness even to the Saviour who had perforce to beg 'and
died in greater poverty than anyone' (B XX 49–50).

The unwary reader might gasp at hearing these words from Langland, for
they were against all that the poet stood for. But they were of course placed
in the mouth of an enemy, and alone of his interviewers Need gets no answer
at all. Instead the dreamer starts at once on his vision of Antichrist.

Why Langland chose to end on this tense and painful note is probably to
be explained by an uncertainty within himself in his own old age. The text
suggests a crisis of confidence here just as it did earlier in his life (B XI), as we

---

[4] For the whole anti-friar discussion see the scholarly work of Szittya, *op.cit. ante*,
esp. ch. 7 'The friars and the end of "Piers Plowman"'.

saw in the chapter on William Langland. In those days he had become aware of the fleeting years. Now there was renewed self-questioning about his mode of life. After the accusing vision of Need had disappeared the air is filled with disease and the thoughts of death. The moment these terrors are taken away Fortune appears, as she did before, with flattering memories of lechery and avarice, and only the shock of self-realization brings the dreamer back to himself.

This crisis (B XX 148–83) is the poet's recognition that Life's laughing imagination of health and pleasure untroubled by holiness or courtesy leads to despair. He comes up short against himself (perhaps again in a mirror), but now he sees a bald and toothless old man. Nature reminds him that, now as always, his only remedy was to learn to love. In this way the poet comes to terms with his ageing self.

William Langland's vision of Antichrist was a nightmare of his old age. But though he accepted what he had become, the friars remained the great enemy. This is an abiding problem of the poem and a special one of its ending, and at the end of this book we still have to face it.

The reader might suppose that old age would have brought greater humility, and that the contrition and confession to which he referred (B XX 213) would have mellowed his attitude. Yet he never repented of his loathing of the mendicants and persisted in viewing the friars as an institution which had become deeply perverse. His opinion was both personal and institutional, but his motives seem intermingled and are hard to disentangle. He never said the friars had been evil from their beginning, and he wrote more than once that Francis and Dominic were men who for love had left their comfortable positions and gone to live humbly on the alms of good people (B XV 419; B XX 252). He thought that even in his own day it might be possible to find a friar of unblemished ideals, unsubverted by avarice.

But he was unrelenting in his criticism of men whose social and intellectual eminence brought them wealth beyond the simple sustenance or 'fyndyng' that once had contented them and might possibly do so again (B XX 384). It is natural to be curious why – apart from the tradition of scholastic quarrels discussed above in Chapter 3 – he should have felt like this.

Teachers and missionaries sometimes become involved with their pupils to the point of feeling almost that they own them. Langland possessed a strong desire to convert others – it is a point of his poem – and the similar vocation of the friars prepared the ground for jealousy. The wider hostility towards friars whipped up again by the FitzRalph campaign in Langland's youth shows that many shared this jealousy even if they did not share Langland's zeal for souls. We cannot know what first sparked Langland's hostility to friars, but FitzRalph certainly fanned it. And as Langland grew older, doubting himself, the 'success' of the friars was undiminished. If he met friars on the street on his way to see his few friends, and noted how the friars' habit was welcomed in many people's homes and indeed in noble households, then the contrast could turn in Langland the knife of bitterness. He was not always welcome. 'Some blamed my life' (B XV 4), not to speak of his disfavour with the idlers who hung round London (C V 3–4).

He might easily enough shrug off lay people who did not want him, but he could not free himself from a sense of inferiority and opposition to the friars. More than a theoretical stance, it was a personal pain.

If Langland was jealous of the friars, he provided a twofold apologia for himself in this last vision. He set himself apart from the clever and successful by numbering himself with the 'holy fools' of whom St Paul speaks; and he deployed the argument that the friars should earn a true living by a suitable craft, namely, they should learn to love.

Langland was deeply preoccupied with 'fools' and referred to them often in the poem.[5] But he was not always writing about the same kind of fool. His age was familiar with feeble-minded folk, fools and madmen who needed the care of the Church (B IX 67f.), and like Piers to whom he ascribed pity on all poor people, Langland's own compassion went out to simple people like this.

But here in the last vision Langland's mind was on the fools for Christ who were to come into the unity of Holy Church and be defended for the love of Piers from the assaulting demons (B XX 74–5; cf. 61–6). These were the truly wise fools of whom St Paul wrote at length to the Corinthians (I Cor. 1:17–31; 3:18–20), the fools who were humble worshippers, believers in the folly of the Cross, not philosophers, not influential and noble, but nonentities who had nothing to boast about but the Lord.

Langland wrote of these fools in this final vision with point and relevance, for he was thinking all this time of the friars. The friars had already dismissed Will as a fool for his *lele speche* (B XI 68–9), or so the poet believed, and it is hard to deny that he saw in himself a spiritual affinity with those who were 'mild and simple' rather than philosophers with sharp wits and tongues. The friars might gloss the Gospel in their own interest, but they had no monopoly of Scripture, which told often of fools in holiness, even like King David himself, a poet who had danced for Yahweh in a loin-cloth and made an exhibition of himself like a buffoon (2 Sam. 6:20–21).

One might go further. Langland as a Pauline fool was one of those late medieval figures who thought to seek God in evangelical simplicity rather than theological subtlety, not unlike Thomas à Kempis who later would argue in *The Imitation of Christ* for trying to love the Trinity rather than to define it. This is not of course to suggest that Langland considered himself a half-wit, however he chose to describe himself in the waking episodes of his poem, since he knew well enough what sort of achievement it was, gloried in

---

[5] On 'fools', see the discussion by E. Talbot Donaldson, *Piers Plowman: The C Text and its poet* (1949 and reprints); also Derek Pearsall, *Piers Plowman: an edition of the C-text* (1978), p. 165 note 105 and p. 167 note 136.

the learning he had – 'the portion of his inheritance' – and even acknowl-
edged his temptations to learn 'all the subtle crafts'. But always at the crucial
moments of his theme he contrived a reduction of complex ideas, like
Indulgences and the Law, to concepts of great simplicity which engage the
heart and the will: 'Do Well', 'forgive', 'love God and your neighbour'. The
fools in the final *Passus* are defenders of an interior spirituality of love
against Dr Flatterer and his kind, who seemed outwardly learned and
capable.

The second part of Langland's apologia for his rejection of the friars was
closely allied with the first. It was the vital requirement to earn a living; and
though he demanded this of the friars he asked it of himself also. 'Learn to
love' was the instruction. Conscience gave the message cheerfully enough to
the friars, who would be given all they needed in the way of food and
clothing, but on the condition 'You give up studying logic, gentlemen, and
learn to love' (B XX 250). For himself too in old age, even as the poem
actually celebrating divine love was almost finished, he made Nature
(*Kynde*) instruct him what craft was best to learn, and having humbly
accepted this he wrote down his own answer, 'learn to love and leave
everything else' (B XX 208).

By the end of *Piers Plowman* we are left with contradictory thoughts about
its author. The last *Passus* is a climax of criticism against the friars, yet also
an exhibition of humility in himself, for he acknowledges in evident sincerity
that he too has the lesson of love still to learn and still begs for grace, as once
long ago he had hoped for grace to begin with (C V 99–101).

The personal hostility to the friars sits with uneasy weight on the conclusion of a long, spiritual poem. That Langland took up ideas which were
part of an angry tradition does not mean that he did not hold them strongly
himself. He was responsible for his own virulence, and a historian may fairly
tax him with it, not for distorting a poem or amusing himself but for
perpetuating a smear across his own face in speaking hatred against a
numerous and dedicated order of men.

Langland accused the friars of cultivating the rich because they lacked
their own endowments; but in refusing lands and lordships they were merely
keeping their own rule, and if they begged successfully instead they can
hardly have been generally disapproved. He accused them of peddling
spiritual privileges like funerals in friars' cemeteries in return for payment,
yet he argued almost in the same breath that money thus spent was
unavailing. Conversely, he said the friars despised the poor but never
followed through his own argument to see that the poor were in his terms not
losing anything worth having. He accused the friars of subverting penance by
making light of sin and restitution, so that men and women fell short in their
repentance. But even a historian may ask how Langland could have known

the truth of such charges, since no-one can know about interior dispositions, much less about the mind of God: it was Langland himself who said only God could see into men's souls.

So however profound Langland may have been as a spiritual writer, it is not easy to acquit him of presumptious judgment of other people's confessions, both as made by penitents and heard by priests.

To Langland the friars could not do right. If they spoke homely sermons to simple parishioners they were being easy-going for gain. If they turned philosopher and speculated about the Divine Essence they were intellectually arrogant. In short, Langland's friars were betrayers of Christ.

Yet his picture does not accord with what we know historically about the friars. We too as historians cannot make moral judgments without the dread of mistake, but the historical sources are persuasive that the friars worked hard in preaching and teaching, threw light on Scripture studies, attracted people to listen to lively sermons, to examine their consciences and confess when they might have stayed away throughout the year in boredom or ignorance, and that for all kinds of reason they helped populate the urban scene with the priests that landlord-monks and country clergy could not so well supply.

In the end a historian may himself confess a certain relief in not having to write the life of a saint. Langland's sarcasm and his obsessions make him historically believable, even while his insights and his poetry enrich our understanding.

THE USE OF TEXTS

Piers Plowman is divided into sections usually called *Passus* (in both singular and plural), of which the B Text contains twenty together with a Prologue. The story moves along through these *Passus* in distinct episodes which could have been used as instalments if the poem was being narrated as a serial.

In this book quotations are usually but not always taken from the B Text. The normal way of citing a passage is therefore to give Version, *Passus* and line, thus:

> . . . and sodeynly me mette
> That Piers the Plowman was peynted al blody . . .   (B XIX 6–7)

> [And suddenly I dreamed that Piers the Plowman was all stained with blood.]

As it is desired that references should be rapidly understood in the context of the present book's argument they are repeated also in modern English where it seems appropriate for the convenience of non-specialists. On some occasions the liberty has been taken of representing an incident or a conversation directly in modern idiom.

The following editions have been used as sources for quotations:

A text: *Piers Plowman: The A version. Will's Vision of Piers Plowman and Do-Well*, ed. G. Kane (University of London, Athlone Press, 1960).

B text: *William Langland: The Vision of Piers Plowman. A complete edition of the B-Text* by A. V. C. Schmidt (Dent: Everyman's Library, 1978 since reprinted with revisions and corrections). Also in paperback.

C text: *Piers Plowman by William Langland: an edition of the C-text* by Derek Pearsall (York Medieval Texts, second series. Edward Arnold, 1978). Also in paperback.

Translations into modern English placed within square brackets are often but not always taken from *Piers the Ploughman: William Langland* translated into modern English with an introduction by J. F. Goodridge, Penguin Books 1959, and subsequently reprinted with revisions.

In Biblical references the *New Jerusalem Bible* has generally been used.

SELECT BIBLIOGRAPHY

Works included in this list fall into two main categories: those which have been especially valuable in the preparation of this book, and those by which the reader may find a way through the vast literature to matters on which he or she wishes to know more. There is, of course, no implied criticism of works omitted from the list below.

For bibliography of bibliographies

Alford, John A. (ed.) *A Companion to 'Piers Plowman'* (University of California Press, 1988).

Adams, Robert, 'The Nature of Need in 'Piers Plowman', *Traditio* 34 (1978), 273–301.

Baker, Timothy, *Medieval London* (1970).

Barney, Stephen A., 'The Plowshare of the Tongue: the progress of a symbol from the Bible to 'Piers Plowman', *Medieval Studies* 35 (Toronto 1973), 261–93.

Barron, Caroline M., 'The parish fraternities of medieval London', in *The Church in Pre-Reformation Society*, ed. Caroline Barron and Christopher Harper-Bill (1985), 13–37.

Bennett, J. A. W., 'Chaucer's Contemporary', in S. S. Hussey (ed.) *Piers Plowman: critical approaches* (1969), repr. in *The Humane Medievalist* (Rome, 1982).

Bishop, Edmund, *Liturgica Historica* (Oxford, 1918).

Bolton, J. L., *The Medieval English Economy, 1150–1500* (2nd ed. 1985).

Bossy, John, *Christianity in the West, 1400–1700* (Oxford, 1985).

Broomfield, F. (ed.), *Thome de Chobham summa confessorum* (Analecta Medievalia Namurcensis 25) (Namur, 1968).

Bullock-Davies, Constance, *A Register of Royal and Baronial Domestic Minstrels, 1272–1327* (1988).

Burrow, J. A., 'Words, works and Will: theme and structure in Piers Plowman', in S. S. Hussey (ed.), *Piers Plowman: critical approaches* (1969).

——, *Ricardian Poetry: Chaucer, Gower, Langland and the 'Gawain' Poet* (1971).

——, 'Langland Nel Mezzo del Camin', in *Medieval Studies for J.A.W. Bennett* (1981), 21–44.

——, 'Autobiographical Poetry in the Middle Ages', *Proceedings of the British Academy* 68 (1982), 389–412.

Burrow, J. A., *Medieval Writers and their work: Middle English Literature and its background, 1100–1500* (Oxford, 1982).

———, *Essays on Medieval Literature* (Oxford, 1984).

———, *The Ages of Man* (Oxford, 1986).

Butler-Bowden, W. (ed.), *The Book of Margery Kempe: a modern version* (Oxford: World's Classics, 1954).

Cargill, Oscar, 'The Langland Myth', *Proceedings of the Modern Language Association* (Baltimore) 50 (1953).

Clark, Francis, *Eucharistic Sacrifice and the Reformation* (1960).

Cloud of Unknowing, The, and other works, Anon., modernized and ed. Clifton Wolters (Penguin Classics, 1978 and repr.).

Coleman, Janet, *English Literature in History, 1350–1400: Medieval Readers and Writers* (1981).

Coleman, Olive, 'Trade and Prosperity in fifteenth-century Southampton', *Economic History Review* 2nd series XXVI No. 1 (August 1963), 9–22.

Copleston, Frederick, *A History of Philosophy*, vol. 3 (Ockham to Suarez) (1953), [esp. chs. 8 and 9 for Ockham on evangelical poverty, and terminist logic in 14th-century Oxford].

Cross, Claire, 'Great Reasoners in Scripture: the activities of women Lollards, 1380–1530', in *Medieval Women*, ed. Derek Baker (Studies in Church History: Subsidia 1. Ecclesiastical History Society, 1978), 359–80.

Denziger, H., *Enchiridion Symbolorum Definitionum et Declarationum de rebus Fidei et Morum*, Editio 24–25 (Herder, Barcelona, 1948).

Donaldson, E. Talbot, *Piers Plowman: the C Text and its poet* (Yale Studies in English 113: New Haven 1949 and repr.).

Du Boulay, F. R. H., 'The Quarrel between the Carmelite friars and the secular clergy of London, 1464–1468', *Journal of Ecclesiastical History* 6 No. 2 (Oct. 1955), 156–74.

———, *The Lordship of Canterbury* (1966).

———, *An Age of Ambition: English society in the late Middle Ages* (1970).

Du Boulay, F. R. H. and Barron, Caroline M. (eds.), *The Reign of Richard II: Essays in Honour of May McKisack* (1971), esp. Beatric White, 'Poet and Peasant', 58–74.

Dyer, Christopher, *Standards of Living in the later Middle Ages* (Cambridge, 1989).

Edwards, J. G., 'Some common petitions in Richard II's first parliament [Oct. 1377],' *Bulletin of the Institute of Historical Research* 26 (1953), 200–13.

Evans, Joan (ed.), *The Flowering of the Middle Ages* (1966).

Goldsmith, Margaret, *The Figure of Piers Plowman: the image on the coin* (Cambridge: D. S. Brewer, 1981).

Goodman, Anthony, 'The piety of John Brunham's daughter, of Lynn', in Medieval Women (as above under Cross, Claire), 347–58.

Gradon, Pamela, 'Langland and the Ideology of Dissent', *Proceedings of the British Academy* 66 (1980), 179–205.

Griffiths, Jeremy, and Pearsall, Derek, *Book Production and Publishing in Britain, 1375–1475* (Cambridge, 1989).

Gwynn, Aubrey, *The English Austin Friars in the time of Wyclif* (Oxford, 1940).

Hamilton Thompson, A., *The Historical Growth of the English Parish Church* (Cambridge, 1913).

——, *The English Clergy and their organization in the later Middle Ages* (Oxford, 1947).

Harwood, Britton J., 'Imaginative in Piers Plowman', *Medium Aevum* 44 (1975), 249–63.

Hatcher, John, *Plague, Population and the English Economy, 1348–1530* (1977).

Hefele, C.-J., and Leclercq, H., *Histoire des Conciles*, V, 2 (Paris, 1913).

Heyworth, Peter L., *Medieval Studies presented to J. A. W. Bennett* (Oxford, 1981).

Hilton, R. H., *A Medieval Society: the West Midlands at the end of the Thirteenth Century* (1966).

Hilton, Walter, *The Ladder of Perfection*, transl. by Leo Sherley-Price (Penguin Classics, 1957 and repr.).

Holmes, G. A., *The Good Parliament* (Oxford, 1975).

Hudson, Anne, *Lollards and their books* (1985).

——, *The Premature Reformation* (1989).

Hussey, S. S. (ed.), *Piers Plowman: critical approaches* (1969).

Julian of Norwich, *Revelations of Divine Love*, modernized by Clifton Wolters (Penguin Classics, 1966 and repr.).

Kane, George, *The Autobiographical Fallacy* (1965).

——, *Piers Plowman: the evidence for authorship* (1965).

Kaske, R. E., 'Langland and the *paradisus claustralis*', *Modern Language Notes* 72 (1957), 482.

Knowles, David, *The Religious Orders in England*, vol. 2, *The End of the Middle Ages* (Cambridge, 1955), esp. 108–111.

——, *The English Mystical Tradition* (1961).

Lambert, Malcolm, *Franciscan Poverty* (1961).

——, *Medieval Heresy* (1977).

Leff, Gordon, *Paris and Oxford Universities in the Thirteenth and Fourteenth Centuries* (New York, 1968).

——, *Heresy in the later Middle Ages*, 2 vols. (Manchester and New York, 1967).

Little, A. G., *Studies in English Franciscan History* (Manchester, 1917).

Little, A. G. and Pelster, F., *Oxford Theology and Theologians in the thirteenth century*, (Oxford Historical Society 96 (1934), 25–64 [for theological training].

Lunt, W. E., *Financial Relations of the Papacy with England, 1327–1534* (Medieval Academy of America, Cambridge, Mass., 1962), [chs. 9 to 12 for detailed treatment of Indulgences in England].

Maguire, Stella, 'The significance of Haukyn, Activa Vita, in Piers Plowman', *Review of English Studies* 25 (1949), 97–109.

Mayer, H. E., *The Crusades* (Engl. transl. Oxford, 1972) [for Indulgences].

Middleton, Anne, 'The Audience and Public of "Piers Plowman"', in Lawton, David (ed.) *Medieval English Alliterative poetry and its literary background* (Cambridge: D. S. Brewer, 1982), 101–23.

Moorman, J. R. H., *Church Life in England in the Thirteenth Century* (Cambridge, 1946).

——, *A History of the Franciscan Order* (Oxford, 1968).

Moss, Douglas, 'The economic development of a Middlesex village [Tottenham]', *Agricultural History Review* 28 (1980), 104–114.

Murray, Alexander, 'Confession as a historical source in the thirteenth century', in Davis, R. H. C. et al. (eds.), *The Writing of History in the Middle Ages: essays presented to Richard William Southern* (Oxford, 1981), 275–322.

Murtaugh, D. M., *Piers Plowman and the Image of God* (Gainesville, Florida, 1978).

Muscatine, Charles, *The Old French Fabliaux* (Yale, 1986).

Myers, Alec R. (ed.), *English Historical Documents*, vol. 6 (1327–1485) (1969).

Orme, Nicholas, *English Schools in the Middle Ages* (1973).

Owst, G. R., 'The "Angel" and the "Goliardys" of Langland's Prologue', *Modern Language Review* 20 (1925), 270–9.

Pantin, W. A., *The English Church in the Fourteenth Century* (Cambridge, 1955).

——, 'Instruction for a devout and literate layman' in J. J. G. Alexander and M. T. Gibson (eds.), *Medieval Learning and Literature* (Oxford, 1976).

Power, Eileen, *The Wool Trade in English Medieval History* (Oxford, 1941).

Prestwich, Michael, *The three Edwards: war and state in England, 1272–1377* (1980).

Putnam, Bertha H., *The Enforcement of the Statute of Labourers during the first decade after the Black Death, 1349–59* (New York, 1908).

Rashdall, Hastings, (ed. F. M. Powicke and A. B. Emden), *The Universities of Europe in the Middle Ages* (1936), vol. 1, esp. 344–97 [for the Mendicants and the University of Paris].

Reeves, Marjorie, *The Influence of Prophecy in the later Middle Ages: a study in Joachimism* (Oxford, 1969).

Richardson, H. G., 'Parish Clergy of the 13th and 14th centuries', *Transactions of the Royal Historical Society*, 3rd series, vol. 6 (1912).

——, 'Business Training in medieval Oxford', *American Historical Review* 46 (1941), 259–80.

Rickert, Edith, 'John But, Messenger and Maker', *Modern Philology* 11 (1913), 1–10.

Ringbom, Sixten, *Icon to Narrative: the rise of the dramatic close-up in fifteenth-century devotional painting* (Åbo, Finland, 1965).

Robinson, F. N. (ed.), *The Works of Geoffrey Chaucer* (2nd ed. 1966).

Rolle, Richard, *The Fire of Love*, transl. and ed. Clifton Wolters (Penguin Classics, 1972 and repr.).

Roskell, J. S., *The Commons and their Speakers in English Parliaments, 1376–1523* (Manchester, 1965).

Rouse, Richard H. and Mary A., 'The Franciscans and Books: Lollard accusations and the Franciscan response', in *From Ockham to Wyclif*, ed. Anne Hudson and Michael Wilks (Studies in Church History, Subsidia 5. Ecclesiastical History Society, 1987), 369–84.

Salter, Elizabeth, *Fourteenth-century English Poetry: contexts and readings* (Oxford, 1983).

Samuels, M. L., 'Langland's Dialect', *Medium Aevum* 54 (1985), No. 2, 232–47.

Scattergood, V. J., 'The Two Ways: an unpublished religious treatise by Sir John Clanvowe', *English Philological Studies* 10 (1967), 33–56.

Shepherd, Geoffrey, 'Religion and Philosophy in Chaucer', in Derek Brewer (ed.), *Geoffrey Chaucer: Writers and their Background* (1974), 262–89.

——, 'Poverty in Piers Plowman', in *Social Relations and Ideas: Essays in Honour of R. H. Hilton*, ed. T. H. Aston et al. (Cambridge, 1983).

Smalley, Beryl, *The Study of the Bible in the Middle Ages* (3rd ed. 1983).

———, 'The Bible and Eternity: John Wyclif's dilemma', *Journal of the Warburg and Courtauld Institutes* 27 (1964), 73–89. [For Oxford's intellectual climate].

Southern, R. W., *Western Society and the Church in the Middle Ages* (Pelican History of the Church 2, Harmondsworth, 1970).

Spearing, A. C., *Medieval Dream Poetry* (Cambridge, 1976).

Swanson, R. N., *Church and Society in late medieval England* (Basil Blackwell, Oxford, 1989).

Szittya, Penn R., *The Antifraternal Tradition in Medieval Literature* (Princeton, 1986).

Tanner, N. P., *The Church in late medieval Norwich, 1370–1532* (Toronto, 1984).

Tentler, Thomas N., 'The Summa for confessors as an instrument of social control', in Charles Trinkaus and Heiko Oberman (eds.), *The pursuit of holiness in late medieval and Renaissance religion* (Leiden, 1974), 103–37.

Thrupp, Sylvia, *The Merchant Class of Medieval London* (Ann Arbor, University of Michigan, 1948).

Titow, J. Z., 'Some differences between manors and their effects on the conditions of the peasant in the thirteenth century', *Agricultural History Review* 10 (1962), 1–13.

Tout, T. F., *Chapters in medieval administrative history*, 6 vols. (Manchester, 1920–33) [esp. vol. 3: administration and politics under Edward III and Richard II].

Walsh, Katherine, *A fourteenth-century scholar and primate: Richard FitzRalph in Oxford, Avignon and Armagh* (Oxford, 1981).

Wilkinson, B., *Constitutional History of Medieval England, 1216–1399*, vol. 3: *the development of the constitution* (1958), [esp. ch. 1, on kingship].

Woodcock, B. L., *Medieval Ecclesiastical Courts in the Diocese of Canterbury* (Oxford, 1952).

Wood-Legh, K. L., *A small household of the fifteenth century* (Manchester, 1956).

Wunderli, Richard M., *London Church Courts and Society on the eve of the Reformation* (Medieval Academy of America, Cambridge, Mass., 1981).

INDEX

Persons living in the Middle Ages are listed by their first names, those in modern times by their surnames. The Select Bibliography is not indexed.

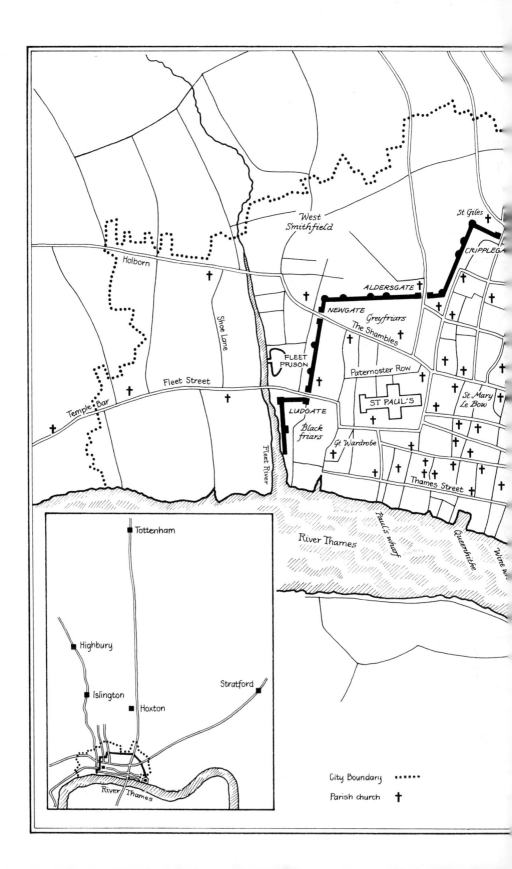

St Giles

CRIPPLEGA

West
Smithfield

ALDERSGATE

Holborn

NEWGATE   Greyfriars

The Shambles

Shoe Lane

FLEET
PRISON

Paternoster Row

Fleet Street

ST PAUL'S

St Mary
Le Bow

Temple Bar

LUDGATE

Black
friars

Gt Wardrobe

Fleet River

Thames Street

River Thames

Paul's wharf

Queenhithe

Wine w

Tottenham

Highbury

Islington

Hoxton

Stratford

River Thames

City Boundary ......

Parish church ✝